LOOK AWAY, DIXIELAND

REFLECTIONS OF A
20th CENTURY SOUTHERN FAMILY

ISBN-10: 1463500688
EAN-13: 9781463500689

LOOK AWAY, DIXIELAND

REFLECTIONS OF A
20th CENTURY SOUTHERN FAMILY

"Old Times There Are Not Forgotten"

Jackson Evans Butterworth, Jr., M.D.

Whereas the live-oak, being a tree indigenous to the soil of our State and especially flourishing along the Coastal plains and islands thereof where the first settlers and founders of this State resided, and which tree is so closely associated with our early history.....

Be it therefore resolved by the House of Representatives of Georgia, the Senate concurring, at the suggestion and request of Edmund Burke Chapter, Daughters of the American Revolution, the live-oak be and the same is hereby adopted as and declared to be the official tree emblematic of the State of Georgia. February 25, 1937

FROM ENGLAND, IRELAND, SCOTLAND, AND FRANCE, THESE FAMILIES CAME TO VIRGINIA, NORTH CAROLINA, SOUTH CAROLINA, AND EVENTUALLY TO GEORGIA. "TO LIVE AND DIE IN DIXIE"

Appreciation: *A work of this order requires many contributions from scores of individuals both living and deceased. Their lives have created the loving environment that makes up our world of family. First I thank my wife, Nancy Godsey Butterworth, who endured my many hours in the basement compiling this information. She patiently proof read the drafts and offered necessary changes. John Butterworth gave me encouragement as well as editorial support without which there would be no book. Living contributors include my brother James Newby Butterworth and cousins Brenda Guinn Coppinger, Nancy Campbell Eaton, William Newby Kelt, JoAnn Butterworth Caton Katnick, Patricia Butterworth Eggers, and Helene and Paul Mewburn. William Evans Butterworth and Amanda Grace Butterworth have contributed their colorful personalities to this effort. Writings and lives of John Evans Butterworth, Buena Vista Wilberth Evans, and David Butterworth add wonderful color to this story. Mr. Walter V. Ball through his excellent genealogical research in his book The Butterworth Family of Virginia and Maryland offered the primary reference for beginning this work. The lives and nurturing of my grandparents, aunts, and uncles which include the families of Butterworth, Evans, Newby, Walden, Campbell, Turner, Gwinn, Forbes, Kelt, Pharr, Tharpe, as well as so many others I cannot list,make up our family group and compose our life's result. I thank all of them for that gift.*

Dedicated to the lives of:

Virgil Ralph and George Wilberth Evans Butterworth

William Franklin and Viola Paulette Walden Newby

Jackson Evans, Sr. and Gertrude Annette Newby Butterworth

May 2011

Table of Contents

Index of Images

Apology

(a reasoned argument or writing in justification....)

Deut. 10   When the LORD your God brings you into the land he swore to your fathers, to Abraham, Isaac, and Jacob, to give you a land with large, flourishing cities you did not build, 11 houses filled with all kinds of good things you did not provide, wells you did not dig, and vineyards and olive groves you did not plant—then when you eat and are satisfied, 12 be careful that you do not forget the LORD, who brought you out of Egypt, out of the land of slavery.

Nights Under a Tin Roof, James Autry

"What are you doing here

In this conference room?

Out of the cotton fields and the red dust

Looking over the coffee and the pads

Lined yellow and legal size

What do you expect me to think

With your country church and preacher man rightness

Nodding at the plan

Smiling at the chart

Acting like the profit margins make a dam

When I know where you come from?

Who do you think you're kiddin'?

The cowshit just off your shoes

Not far enough from overalls

To be happy in a collar

With GQ in the briefcase

And a charge at Saks"

These are markedly different passages. One is Biblical, warning the Israelites not to forget their Lord and his guidance from slavery to the Promised Land. One is a poem, crudely reminding modern man where he originated.Both relate to a regard for our God and our Ancestors who prepared for us the world in which we live. We are blessed to have relatives who endured times and hardships before us and helped develop our current circumstances of much easier life styles filled with opportunities. We also recognize that our God created and guided those individuals. Look Away, Dixieland can help us to remember and reflect on both of those blessings.

For several years I have planned to organize my thoughts of the past with information given to me of our family history. Fragments of information and stories we have been told about our Grandfathers and Grandmothers and where they lived in the past drifted in my consciousness in an unorganized pattern. I have been given many notes, letters, scrapbooks, bibles, and oral stories that all tell a part of this history. Our family treasure has lived in boxes for many years. I hope this effort at consolidation will be meaningful to those who become interested in their origins in days to come. Our story, and it is all ours, begins by listing our ancestors who came to America three or four centuries ago. It gives fragments of references of those ancestors who left Scotland, England, Ireland, France, and Scandinavia and settled in America. We are a composite of all these countries' histories and influences. Our DNA has been diluted with contributions from the British Isles and Western Europe and does not give us any immediate bonding to one European locale. But the connections we do know make the history of those regions seem closer to us. If we admit to any majority heritage it would be to the Islands of Great Britain and to the French Huguenots.

This work will begin with the Butterworth family, since that is my surname, and then follow with the Newby family. There are many branches from both of these starting points. Many, many, very admirable individuals are contained in this narrative and they contributed to the formation of their communities, their nation, and especially their families. We can be very proud of this heritage. As expected, there is the occasional individual who did not find the existing mores and laws to be their guide, but that makes history more interesting. If we all followed one pattern, it would make a boring story indeed. The two families depicted in this narrative both settled in the state of Georgia, one North and one Middle Georgia. I will review the lineage, site of origin, and passage to America of both groups with descriptions and family stories.

Lists of names and dates are available on other sites like Ancestry.com. When possible I will try to relate the family to events and trends of the time that may have influenced their actions. I am fortunate to have contributions from Cousins who are great storytellers. I appreciate their memories and perspectives. If this story is not recorded in some fashion, then we will lose our family heritage. If we preserve our heritage, then we can go proudly into tomorrow knowing from where we originated and how we fit into the cycle of history. Hopefully that knowledge will give us strength and confidence by knowing our forefathers and mothers met challenges equal to those of our times and succeeded. Read on and let me know what we need to add the next time around.

Part I
Butterworth and Related Families

Butterworth

The Butterworth family reaches far back into history. The branches that the family takes through marriages are rich and colorful. The site of the Butterworths in England is in the Township of Butterworth near Rochdale, Lancaster County, in Western England. Reginald de Butterworth built the original Butterworth Hall in that area. That is most likely the site of our origin. In Appendix I. are some details on the further origin of the name. We share genetic material with relatives from Scotland and other areas of the British Isles. Several family lines will be discussed later but I wish to mention the Wheeler family at this juncture.

Wheeler

John Wheeler was one of the early settlers of Maryland. We do not know the date of his arrival in that colony but it is likely to be in 1652. He has been located in Charles County that year. He arrived on the ship <u>Thomas and Mary</u> with Captain Mitchell. John was a servant of Capt. Mitchell on that voyage. John rose to be a prominent citizen of Charles County and was Major of the Militia, a large landowner, and a Justice of the Court. He was a Roman Catholic. Maryland was known to be a religiously tolerant colony under Lord Baltimore. Lord Baltimore, a Catholic, struggled to maintain possession of Maryland during the English Civil War by trying to convince Parliament of his loyalty by appointing a Protestant, William Stone, as his governor. Baltimore lost control of the colony for a brief time, however, due to Puritan pressure during the rule of Oliver Cromwell. He regained the colony in 1657, after signing a treaty with Virginia Governor Richard Bennett. It was during another religious conflict, 1689, that John Wheeler was removed as Major of the Militia and relieved of his position in Court. In 1692 he was put out of the list of taxables and made levy free for the future because of his service and his age. John had a large family and was the great grandfather of Jane Wheeler who married Isaac Butterworth. That would make him my 8[th]great-grandfather. This Wheeler family was important in the settlement of Maryland and our young country. Walter V. Ball has written extensively on this family in his Wheeler Family Book of Maryland. He contracted genealogical research in England on John Wheeler but the specific site of the Wheeler's in England has not been identified.

Clement

The Clement family married with the Butterworths twice in the 18th Century. They are still a prominent family in Pittsylvania County, Virginia. The story of Benjamin will be described later as we review his home and Indian fighting service. We have traced his line to Robert Clements born in 1460 in Leicestershire, England. Jeremiah Clement, born in 1607 in London, England to Jeffrey and Elizabeth, came to America with his widowed mother, landing at Jamestown, 1611. Some researchers claim a relationship to Samuel L. Clements, known to the world as Mark Twain but the connection is not clear to me. Jeremiah Clement represented James City County in the House of Burgesses in 1641. He probably died before Surry was made a County. Jeremiah would be my 10th Great Grandfather.

The Evans, Brooke, Knox, and Garrison families came from the Lowland Scots. With the exception of the Garrisons, they migrated to the Ulster Plantation in Northern Ireland and then to America. These Scots-Irish were some of the primary builders of America during the 18th Century. Wales, Western England, and the Netherlands hold extensions for us also. My paternal DNA study, run by the National Geographic lab, showed ancient relationships in the British Isles and parts of France. That matches what we know of our relations. We descend from the Butterworth, Evans, Brooke, Wheeler, Clement, Knox, Garrison, Hughes, and many other names to form our genome of this century. And this mixture continues with each generation. So let us embark on a review of some of these people.

Isaac Butterworth

We begin our primary surname family with **Isaac Butterworth** who arrived in America sometime before 1694. Recall that Jamestown was founded in 1607 and Plymouth Rock in 1620. Those dates relate only to the very first landings at those sites. Following them came the settlers who grew and extended our country. While not the first, Isaac arrived early into a frontier that was offering opportunities as well as challenges to immigrants from the Old World. We have information in Maryland records of his doing business in tobacco in 1694. He was born in 1674 so he traveled from his origin and later entered business by age 20 years. We presume he was born in England although we do not have firm evidence. His sister, Hannah, was in Maryland at that time also. Henry Butterworth was identified in Maryland at the time of the recording of Isaac and it is likely that Henry was the father of Isaac and Hannah.

I engaged a professional genealogist, Peter Wilson Coldham of Surrey, England, in 1980. He failed to definitely identify Isaac and Hannah in Rochdale Parish, the home site of almost all Butterworths in England. Additionally I corresponded with David Butterworth many times and he presented me with in-depth works on the Butterworth family in England. He could not find their origin either. These investigations were in 1970-1990. Perhaps Isaac, Hannah, and Henry along with others, left

Rochdale and went to Ireland with the Ulster Plantation movement, or took a side journey to the Caribbean islands as many did. Maybe the Rochdale parish records were lost or burned. If they went first to foreign sites other than leaving directly from Rochdale, discovery is more difficult.

At any rate we know that Isaac married Esther Clark and his sister Hannah married John Webster. Isaac owned land in Baltimore County Maryland, farmed tobacco, and registered deeds and business transactions. Any other picture of Isaac must be left to our imagination and our knowledge of Maryland during those years of early America. Isaac died in 1728. To date we have no definite proof of the origin of Isaac and Hannah but assume they hail from Rochdale Parish, England located in Lancaster, Western England. There seems to be a preponderance of evidence to this conclusion.

One theme common to the Butterworth family and to many families of the time is the closeness of family members in their homesteads, work, and migrations. Our families continued to retain this proximity and mutual support until very recent generations. The Butterworth family and its ramifications were very close as evidenced by records of when and where they moved. There were always documented affiliations with relatives until recent 20th century society changes.

Family information is well documented and researched in the book by Walter V. Ball, of Chevy Chase Maryland whose mother was a Butterworth. Walter was an excellent researcher and genealogist who published the sentinel book of our family titled The Butterworth Family of Maryland and Virginia. Mr. Ball personally visited with my grandmother, Mrs. V. R. Butterworth at 847 Confederate Avenue in Atlanta on more than one occasion. Mr. Ball has also written another entire book on the Webster family.

Isaac Butterworth, Junior

Isaac Butterworth Junior, b. 1704, lived in Baltimore County Maryland until his death about 1774. He did not create records for us to discover but he did own considerable land. We presume he farmed tobacco which was the cash crop of the time in America. While in Maryland, the family owned land plots with the romantic names of Isaac's Lot, The Addition, Roses Green, Isaac's Inheritance, and Maiden's Bower-over 1400 acres in all. Other land plots named in the wills include the Butterworth Plantation, Uncle's Goodwill, and Three Sisters. Isaac married **Jane Wheeler** who was probably his cousin. She held the same name of the family his aunt Hanna married.

Benjamin Butterworth

Isaac's son Benjamin emigrated from Maryland to Virginia, presumably for better farming opportunities. The definite date of that move is not known but is estimated to be about 1764.

James Leyburn in the outstanding work on Scots Irish immigrations describes the agricultural incentive for migrations of the time.

> *"The opening years of the eighteenth century saw a gradual exhaustion of soil on tobacco plantations both on the Eastern Shore and across the Chesapeake. With this decline of prosperity based upon the staple, those enterprises which had supported English and Scottish traders and manufacturers also suffered. Inevitably the population declined as people began a steady movement northward on the eastern Shore. Economically, it was a movement from plantation services to small farming; geographically, it was a movement toward the Head of Chesapeake where the Susquehanna empties into the bay, and where both Pennsylvania and Delaware make boundaries for Maryland's northeastern county of Cecil."*

Perhaps the Butterworths were caught up in this land depletion and crop change. Obviously something made them give up their holdings and move to new frontiers and opportunities. The route they took to Virginia is under investigation today.

Benjamin Butterworth Sr., son of Isaac Jr., moved to Bedford County Virginia ca. 1767 and bought a plot of land on the south side of Seneca Creek. This is now, 2010, located in Campbell County VA. Jim Butterworth and I visited this area and walked the land in 2010. The land is owned by a gentleman with the quaint name of Billy Joe Poindexter. He and his grandson took us to the site, showed us Seneca creek, and the Staunton River which borders his land.

Fig.1   Seneca Creek, Campbell County Virginia

This is a beautiful site and the owner has created a camping site on the bank of the Staunton River. A large island is in the middle of the river and is the property of this gentleman. He pastures cattle on the island. There is a ford to the island for passage. He rents a portion to a group of Mennonites who use the island for forage also. On one site of the river is a dredging plant siphoning silt from the river bottom for gravel and sand.

Seneca creek is a large creek and an abandoned railroad trestle crosses it. One can see how the river could have been used in the 1700s for produce transportation and travel up or down stream. Benjamin, living on this site, may have courted his wife by boat as she lived with her father just up the river.

Fig. 2 Seneca Creek Trestle 2010

Benjamin married a young girl named **Elizabeth Clement** who lived in the home where her father **Benjamin Clement**, my 6th great grandfather, built Clement Hill which exists in some disrepair in 2010.

Fig.3 Clement Hill, Pittsylvania, County, Virginia, 2010 Home of CPT. Benjamin Clement 1750.

Benjamin Clement was a Captain in the Halifax County Virginia Ranger militia during the French and Indian war. The History of Pittsylvania County, VA describes Captain Benjamin Clements conducting business and living as a neighbor to a Mr. Smith. During the Revolutionary war Benjamin Clement, along with Colonel Charles Lynch for whom Lynchburg, VA is named, devised a method of manufacturing gunpowder from the droppings found in meat curing sheds. They together provided the military with essential gunpowder for the conflict. Benjamin also devised tunnels and escape routes for his wife and family on the Clement Hill site. This was part of a defense from Indians when he was away. He transported his tobacco and other produce down the Staunton River to market on occasions in addition to being away on his Ranger missions. There is much rich history of this large family in the Virginia archives.

Stephen Butterworth 1769-1847

Benjamin and Elizabeth, who died young, had several children and our line stems from son **Stephen** who married another Clement girl, **Rachel.** She was the daughter of Isaac Clement, a brother of Stephen's mother Elizabeth. Following the death of Benjamin Butterworth, Stephen and Rachel inherited land which was contested by the second wife, Sarah. Their inheritance was upheld by the courts of the time. They subsequently sold their Virginia land on Seneca Creek and moved to Greenville District of South Carolina before 1794. Stephen purchased lands from his brothers-in-law in the Pendleton District of SC on the waters of Broad Mouth Creek and the Saluda River. He is listed as purchasing from Edward Smith of Pendleton District 340 acres on the North side of the Saluda River on 18 Dec. 1797. Stephen sold his land in SC in 1818 and on that date Hall County Georgia was formed from Cherokee Indian lands. He is shown in the census of Hall County for 1820. On Feb. 1824 Stephen purchased 247 acres in Hall County on the branch of Barkers Creek and waters of Little River adjacent to land he owned. His wife Rachael died sometime during this interlude. Stephen did have slaves during this period and in the 1830 census Stephen and Rachel Clements had several children. A son **Isaac Clement Butterworth** is my 3rd.great-grandfather

Isaac Clement Butterworth 1800-18//

Isaac Clement, my 3rd. great-grandfathermarried **Parkey Pride Hix** December 20, 1820 in Hall County GA. He died after having a large family. His family is buried in the Lebanon Methodist Cemetery in Gillsville, Hall County, Georgia. Isaac is buried in Talladega Alabama. His son James Marion Butterworth lived in that county with many family members. James M. was a Private in the 31st Alabama Infantry as were many other Butterworths and Joneses, their relatives. James was wounded and reported missing at Baker's Creek and subsequently was captured at Champion Hills. He was imprisoned at Fort Delaware in Delaware City. He died shortly after capture while in the hospital. The son of the marriage of Isaac C. and Parkey Pride which relates to our branch is **John Bevel Butterworth**, b. 23 Sept 1821 and died April 20, 1898.

John Bevel Butterworth, 1821-1898.

John Bevel lived in Hall County but enlisted in the 31st ALA Infantry in Talladega, ALA. He married **Martha Center** 7/28/1828 and Christian Harriet Jones in 1853.

John Bevel, my 2nd great-grandfather served in the 31st ALA infantry, CSA along with his son John and rose to the rank of Company 1st CPL. He surrendered with his company when it stacked arms at Greensboro (April 26, 1865), as part of Pettus' brigade.

Fig.4 John Bevel Butterworth

Fig.5 John Bevel Butterworth

Muster Roll, 31ˢᵗ Alabama Infantry

BUTTERWORTH, A. J., Co. "F"

BUTTERWORTH, G. W., Co. "F"

BUTTERWORTH, J. B., Co. "F"

BUTTERWORTH, J. B., Co. "F", Cpl.

BUTTERWORTH, J. M., Co. "F"

BUTTERWORTH, Lewis N., Co. "F"

BUTTERWORTH, M. R., Co. "F"

BUTTERWORTH, T. N., Co. "F"

I am unclear of the relationship with the Talladega area but there were other family members who migrated to that area as he had sons in the region at the time of the war. John Bevel moved back to Hall County after the war and is buried with his family in the Lebanon Methodist Cemetery in Gillsville, Hall County, GA. A large number of the family was in that county and John Bevel went to Alabama to join the Regiment his family served. His son was one of the enlisted men in the 31ˢᵗ Infantry.

James Henry Butterworth 1850-1899

The fourth child of John Bevel and Parkey Pride Hix was **James Henry Butterworth**, b. Dec. 12,1850 in Hall County, GA and died April 02, 1899 in Canton, Cherokee, GA. He was my great grandfather.

Cherokee County was created in 1831 from Carroll, DeKalb, Gwinnett, Hall, and Habersham. In 1840 the population was only 5,895. A gold lottery brought settlers flowing into the county from 1832. The Land Lottery of 1838 also lured settlers to the Cherokee area. The increase after that was due not to such artificial stimulation but to the inherent advantages of the county according to Rev. Lloyd Marlin in his History of Cherokee County. Roads were beginning to open up, law and order was well established, the land showed productiveness, and the Indians had been removed to the West. These are cited as reasons that **James Henry Butterworth** may have left Hall County for Cherokee County and new opportunities.

James Henry married **Sarilda (Cirilda) Ann Hughes** who was born in Cherokee County July 27, 1852 and died January 12, 1925. James died at the age of 49 leaving many children. Sarilda managed those children by keeping her family in close proximity and having them share in the household duties. In the 1870 census there were two members of the Center family aged 70 and 59 living with James and Sarilda. They were apparently related to John Bevel through Martha Center, perhaps cousins of James Henry. In 1880 James Henry was 28 years old and working for wages.His wife was 25 years old. They had four children. In 1900 after James' death Sarilda lived with six children, the youngest being four years. Family history relates that James Henry died from pneumonia after helping to save individuals caught in a flood. My grandfather, Virgil, said that his father could not swim but he was quoted that he could "walk on the bottom" if necessary. One can see the closeness of family in these reports. It likely was necessary because of economic conditions but it functioned to preserve families and individuals.

Sarilda Ann Hughes, our great grandmother was born in Cherokee County. Her great grandfather, **James Hughes**, (App.VI) emigrated from Wales and fought in the American Revolution. **Sarilda** managed her household with several children and enlisted the assistance of her daughter Emma to help with some of the children. Emma lived next door after marriage as indicated in the census lists. James and Sarilda had eleven children in their 28 years of marriage. My grandfather, Virgil Ralph, was one of these eleven children in the 1910 census. At the age of 23, Virgil and his wife **George Evans** lived with Virgil's sister, Emma Fowler, along with his son, my father **Jackson Evans Butterworth**.

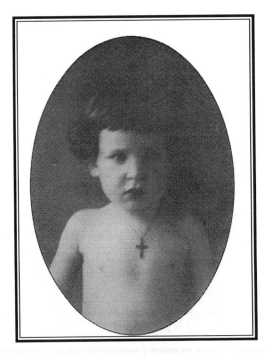

Fig.6 Jackson Evans Butterworth Sr., age 1 year- 1909

At this point our story will move to more current times with descriptions of the life and times of Virgil and George Butterworth and George's relatives.

George Washington Evans

Great-grandfather George Washington Evans was a man of some prominence in Canton, Ga. As a very young man he served in the 12th Regiment of Georgia Cavalry in the War Between the States. At his enlistment for service he was the age of 16-17 years. The situation in his county was difficult with General Sherman marching into the area and terrorizing families. Initially he enlisted in Col. B. F. McCollum's Company A, transferred to Hunicutt's Company B, and then the outfit was converted to Johnson's 12th Regiment of Georgia Cavalry. The story of McCollum's Brigade is complicated and colorful. Whether George Evans was party to the raids of the Scouts is not known. However I think it interesting to review the stories told about McCollum's outfit.

Fig.7 Col. B.F. McCollum of McCollum's Scouts

McCollum's Scouts

"Since no battle of importance between Confederate and Union forces occurred in Cherokee County, it is of especial interest to note the "unofficial" warfare which took place in the county.

Most worrisome to Northern forces of all guerilla fighters in North Georgia was probably a small band of Southern sympathizers, called" McCollum's Scouts," which originated and operated chiefly in Cherokee County during the closing year of the war, and which had the aim of thwarting Sherman's foraging squads and the local Union sympathizers.

Not outlaws, McCollum's Scouts were a peculiar product of the local environment with its mixed sentiment. To some persons they seemed murderous fiends; to others they were avenging angels. It depended on the viewpoint.

References to guerilla bands in the Civil War are plentiful; authoritative accounts of them are not; and it is fortunate that details concerning McCollum's Scouts have been preserved by a distinguished son of Cherokee and a historian at heart, Judge William A. Covington, now of Atlanta. Of his own family's connection with this phase of the war, Judge Covington relates that two of his distant kinsmen were executed by Scouts; on the other hand, his grandfather's farm on Shoal Creek near Waleska was raided by Sherman's foragers, who "made a clean sweep of everything they could carry off, my grandfather being old and his sons being with Lee in Virginia." The following full account of McCollum's Scouts, published here for the first time and of definite historical importance, is from the pen of Judge Covington:

"There were many people in the hill country of Cherokee, Bartow, and Gordon Counties who, while having sympathies with one side or the other, did not join either the Union or Confederate armies and who resisted conscription.

"As Sherman, in the spring of 1864, pressed forward from Chattanooga to Atlanta, he passed down through Bartow and terrorized sympathizers to both North and South. Georgia Governor Brown authorized units to become Militia of the State of Georgia to protect the raids.

{See Judge Covington's account of McCollum's Scouts in History of Cherokee County Rev. Lloyd Marlin and Appendix V. of this work.}

George Washington Evans, for years after the War, operated a livery stable in Canton, GA and was considered a community leader. He was a devoted father to his daughters and provided for them all his life.

MANY CITIZENS OF THE COUNTY will recognize in this above
picture, taken more than twenty-five years ago, the faces of a number of men prominent in Canton and Cherokee County during the
last century. In the front row (left to right) are Odum W. Pittman,
William A. Teasley Sr., Judge James R. Brown, Ben F. Terry Sr.
(kneeling), W. M. Ellis, George W. Brooke, M. A. Lacey, and W. H.
Ponder. In the back row (left to right) are J. E. Hawkins, County
W. Evans, Dr. J. M. Turk, George I. Teasley, a Mr. Williams, D. H.
Attaway, and W. T. McCollum. The old building represented in the
picture was an outbuilding that stood near the old home of Governor Brown in Canton, in what is now Brown Park.

Fig 8. Cherokee County Georgia Leaders ca. 1907

Fig.9 Canton home of George Washington Evans and the childhood home of George Wilberth Evans Butterworth.

Fig 10 George Washington Evans

Virgil Ralph Butterworth 1888-1955

My Grandfather, **Virgil Ralph**, was occupied as a Stone Cutter at the age of 13 years in 1900. He obviously began work at an early age and this likely was a necessity because of the death of his father who left a large family.

John Patrick Butterworth, 1875-1910, was one of Virgil's brothers. He died relatively young. His children were Ralph, Buena, and John Evans. They were raised by Naomi Arwood, a maternal aunt. His obituary states he died in Johnson's Sanitarium in Atlanta after a short stay. He had sudden onset of heart failure. Patrick was a businessman in Canton and member of the Orange Lodge No.39 I.O.O.F. who conducted the services.

Patrick operated the Canton Bottling Works with W.W. Fincher in 1910.

Fig. 11 John Patrick Butterworth

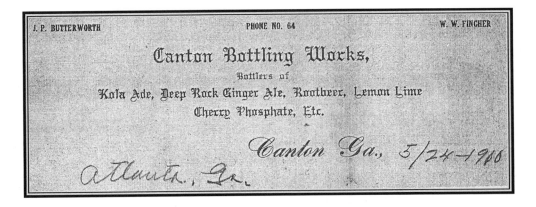

He married Elizabeth Evans, daughter of G.W. Evans. This bonded the Evans and Butterworth families as Virgil Married Lizzie's sister, George Wilberth. He was my Great Uncle and his children were double first cousins with my Father.

We don't know much about Virgil's life in Canton and Cherokee County. Family stories note that he played baseball which was a popular sport in the north Georgia towns. I do know he played trombone in the Canton City band and have attached a photo of that group. How he learned the instrument and what stimulated his musical interest would be a great story.

Fig. 12 Canton City Band ca. 1900

Virgil Ralph is in the middle with the Trombone. The occasion for the photo is unknown.

Virgil worked in the Stone Design or Marble and Granite production business since the age of 13 years. He rose to become a designer and a supervisor of men, a craftsman himself. Marble and Granite design and fabrication was his profession his entire life. He worked for the Dixie Marble and Granite Company in Atlanta for several years.

"The marble businesses which thrived and were a vital part of Cherokee's economy in the early part of the century were both wholesale and retail fabricators using stone from neighboring Pickens County. In 1892 Thomas M. Brady Sr. opened the Georgia Marble Finishing Works in Canton. This was a 'finishing" plant producing monuments. Blocks of marble quarried at Tate were shipped to Canton, sawn, polished, carved, and sold to retailers through the United States. A very high quality workmanship characterized the memorials from this plant which employed skilled designers and carvers. By 1910 there were about a dozen plants in operation in Cherokee, located in Canton and Ball Ground, ranging in size from one man operations to shops employing 100-150 men. Glimpses of Cherokee County, Cherokee *County Historical Society*

Fig.13 Canton Marble Company

Fig.14 Virgil Ralph Butterworth

Virgil worked for a time in the Murphy/Andrews section of North Carolina. I don't know the details of his employment but his family remained in Atlanta on Confederate Avenue. I have a copy of his fishing and trout license for that time in NC. I remember his taking my first pet, a Cocker Spaniel named Ginger, back to N.C with him much to my distress. The dog must have been ill. We lived in Marietta at that time so he must have worked there in the 1940s.

Big Daddy, the grandchildren's name for Virgil, was a quiet, calm, and capable individual. He and his sons-in-law built a screened sun porch on the rear of the Confederate Ave home. It encompassed the entire rear of the house and was floored with a mosaic of marble he obtained from the company. It was built entirely by Fred Turner, Virgil, and M.O. Campbell. This served as a delight to the family for the remaining years.

I remember Big Daddy peeling apples for me and himself. He always had a small very sharp knife in his pocket. This practice was passed on to my dad, Jack, who always carried one with just the same sharpness. I remember buying Dad and myself a special knife before I left for Vietnam. I have his today, but mine was stolen at a medical clinic visit in Quang Tin City. When I visited for a summer sojourn with Big Mamma and Big Daddy for a week in the summer, Big Daddy would come home from work and sit on the front porch and read the Atlanta Journal. Later he watched the news on WSB TV with a 7 inch black and white unit.

Virgil married into the large and prominent family of G. W. Evans of Canton. The entire family moved from Canton, GA to Atlanta about 1918. They lived together on Crew Street just west of downtown Atlanta. I visited there as a college student at Emory in the 50's. We had a work day at a Children's home on Crew Street. There was urban renewal in progress then but the remaining houses were large with vast yards. I do not know if any of these were the family's home. They lived there only a short time.

Virgil and George Wilberth lived for several years with his father –in – law, George Washington Evans in a large house on Delta Place, Atlanta after moving from Crew Street.

Fig.15 Delta Place Style House

The photo is not the family house but represents the same style according to Cousin Helene and Paul Mewburn, whose grandmother Ada Evans Mills lived on Delta Place... Below is an actual picture of the house of William and Ada Evans Mills. Ralph, Buena, and John Evans were reared there with Aunt Naomi Arwood, a widow nurse, to manage them.

Additional family members lived nearby...

{Aunt Milam and Uncle Jim Jones, along with Lillian, lived down on Edgewood Avenue, a little over a block from Delta Place. Carlisle and Martha, along with Larry and Sharon lived upstairs in the two-story, more like a duplex. The home was owned by two bachelor brothers, John and George Farmer.

Aunt Milan died of heart failure, January 27, 1937. Uncle Jim died, December 27, 1947. Lillian died July 29, 1994.} Helene Mewburn

Fig.16 Dan Mills, Buena Butterworth, Buena Vista Evans

My dad and his cousin Wilberth Mills were said to talk and joke while washing dishes through windows open to each other in the neighboring houses. The family continued to live close together leaving many fond memories for the young people.

Fig.17 Delta Place home William and Ada Mills

Inman Park, the site of their home on Delta Place, was the first planned residential suburb developed in Atlanta. Its promoter, Joel Hurt, was one of the city's most important early builders. Improvements to the district, such as streets, a park, part of Atlanta's first electric streetcar line, landscaping and tree planting were well underway by the time the first lots were put up for auction in 1889, officially opening the development of the Inman Park suburb. http://www.nps.gov/nr/travel/atlanta/inm.htm

{Hello Jack, I believe I have found the information you and I were looking for regarding the year our family moved from Canton to Atlanta. I was searching through some old pages of a journal Aunt Naomi left to my Mother to find the answers to some questions Nan had asked me and came across a copy of the obituary of G. W. Evans. It said "...he retired from active business in 1918 (in Canton) and removed to Atlanta to make his home." This would be about what we had decided, would it not? We knew our parents were children when they moved and in 1918 my Mother would have been 8 years old and Uncle Jack 10. So now we know for sure! It feels so good for me to know where to find things. My cleaning out and organizing seems to be paying off. Hope all is good with you and family. Keep in touch. Love, Brenda}

Brooke/Knox Families

George Wilberth Evans Butterworth, my Grandmother, was a descendant of the family of Joseph Knox and Malissa Brooke Knox through her mother Buena Vista Wilberth Knox Evans. Joseph's wife Malissa Brooke was the daughter of James Prescott Brooke who was born on the ship Volunteer in route from Larne, Ireland to Charles Town, S. C. in 1795. These families were Scots-Irish with documented histories of emigration fromScotland to Ulster Ireland, and then America. I estimate the Knox arrival in America about 1770. The Knox family moved from Mecklenburg, NC to Rutherford NC.

FIRST SCHOOL TEACHER and his wife. Joseph Knox, pioneer settler of Sutallee District, was Cherokee County's first school teacher. His picture is shown here together with that of his wife who was a daughter of John P. Brooke, one of the three founders of Canton.

Fig.18   Joseph and Malissa Knox

HOME OF AN EARLY SETTLER. This old house, built in 1837 by Joseph Knox, early pioneer and first school-teacher of Cherokee County, was one of the first homes built in Sutallee District. It is still standing.

Fig.19   Home of Joseph Knox

After arriving in Charles Town, S.C., the Brooke family migrated to Abbeville and Pendleton District from Charles Town. The History of Cherokee County, Georgia by Rev. Lloyd Marlin states that John Prescott Brooke family moved from South Carolina to Hall County, Georgia and then to Cherokee County Ga. John was twice in the legislature from Hall County, was a militia colonel, and an inspector-general for Hall, Habersham, and Rabun Counties. He helped establish Canton Georgia and was the second sheriff of the county in 1833. He is buried at Sixes Cemetery.

Fig.20 *John Prescott Brooke*

Fig.21 *Hester Bennett Brooke*

{In 1763 the province (South Carolina) became interested in attracting settlers into the up –country and a bounty was offered to stimulate immigration. A "headright" of a hundred acres for each man with fifty acres for each woman and child was offered. The government supplied indispensable implements for agriculture. (Edward McCrady, History of South Carolina under the Royal Government, 1719-1776.) This possibly was an incentive for the Knox and Brooke families to move to the up country.}

Garrison Family

Another family we proudly claim as relatives is that of the **Garrisons**. Five Garrison brothers emigrated from Scotland in 1700 and landed on the coast of Delaware. They secured a land grant on the borders of Maryland from King George III of England. Only three of the names are known-David, Christopher, and Jedadiah Garrison. One brother married a relative of Pocahontas. Hostile Indians burned the brothers out and they separated. David's descendants settled in Greenville, Anderson and surrounding counties. Our David Garrison married Elizabeth Barksdale of Barksdale Depot, VA. They bought a large tract of land on the Saluda River between Piedmont and Pelzer in Greenville

County, SC. David operated a grist mill and tavern in Piedmont, S.C.until he sold it to a textile industrialist. David and Elizabeth are buried on this land.

Elizabeth Barksdale was a sister of Collier and Nathaniel Barksdale whose father emigrated from England in the 18th cn. And settled near Barksdale Depot VA. The Barksdales are another of our related families who prominently established themselves in our developing country.

David Garrison, my 4th great-grandfather, served in the Maryland artillery during the Revolutionary war in the First Company of Matrosses, Province of Maryland. His enlistment date was January 24, 1776. He was born in West Salem, NJ in 1745. They had many children but our line comes through their seventh son, Nehemiah Garrison, who was our 3rd Great Grandfather. Nehemiah was also in the military. He married Sarah "Sallie" Evans the daughter of Judge Phillip Evans. Later they moved to Hall County Georgia and were among the first settlers in that area. According to tradition, Nehemiah helped to "lay out" the city of Gainesville, Georgia. He was a Captain in the War of 1812 and for several years represented Hall County in the State Senate. Captain Nehemiah Garrison was in command of the detachment of soldiers when Fort Daniel was erected. During the War of1812, forts were erected at points along the frontier since the Indians were aiding the British. Hog Mountain was the most western point on the frontier and many families lived in the section.

Fig.22 Georgia Marker-Ft. Daniel

Hog Mountain was selected as a site to locate a fort. That fort was garrisoned by officers, spies, and volunteers during the war. It was named Fort Daniel.

It later became necessary to establish another fort farther into Indian Territory and George R. Gilmer, who was subsequently Governor of Georgia, was ordered to advance into the territory west of Hog Mountain. Gilmer wrote in his book, <u>Georgians</u>, that his appointed station was on the banks of the Chattahoochee 30 miles beyond the frontiers of the state, near an Indian town. This became known as "Standing Peachtree" and a fort was erected there.

Fig. 23 Georgia Marker Ft. Peachtree

This new fort required building a road from Fort Daniel to Standing Peachtree. Thus the new road was called Peachtree Road from the time it was opened for travel. The original road extended from Hog Mountain to Standing Peachtree. It is likely, according to historians, that Captain Nehemiah Garrison, Commandant of the detachment of soldiers when Ft. Daniel was erected, was responsible for the creation of this road. (Gainesville Daily Times Editorial)

In the early 1830's Nehemiah and his family moved to Cherokee County, Georgia where his son John Barksdale Garrison and family had been living for several years among the Indians. Father and son lived in the Fort Buffington area and helped to move the Indians in 1838

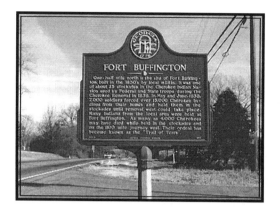

Fig.24 Nehemiah Garrison Marker

A marker erected by the United Society of the War of 1812 for Nehemiah Garrison is in the City
Cemetery of Canton, Georgia.

George Wilberth Evans (Butterworth)

Virgil and George purchased a house on Confederate Avenue in Atlanta and lived there until an old age. The entire time in Atlanta, they had family living in close proximity. At Delta Place they lived next door to other Evans daughters, Ada and Naomi, along with John Evans, Agnes, and Ralph, the children of Pat and Lizzie Butterworth, both deceased. Wilberth Mills, daughter to Ada lived with this family as William Mills, her father, had died. On Confederate Avenue they had their daughters Sue within walking distance, Billie at home, and Mary and Fred across town.

Fig.25 Big Mama's Back Yard

Back row: Sue Gwinn, Gertrude Butterworth with Jimmy, M.O. Campbell, Mary Turner, Billy Campbell. Front Row: Brenda Gwinn, Big Mamma,? Lynn Turner, Jackie, Jim's mount ca 1945

Their son, Jack lived with them until married and then returned for a six month stay in 1938 before moving to Marietta, Ga. The family was obviously close and lived well together. During WWII two of Virgil and George's daughters lived in a three bedroom house on Confederate Avenue with the two of them. Each daughter had children with a total of at least six individuals together in a small house.

Fig.26 347 Confederate Avenue, Atlanta, Ga (Virgil and George)

Virgil and George found their happiness in the lives of their family. They provided a base for their children as well as a home for cousins when desired. Their influence on their progeny is unlimited.

The following is a story written by Brenda Gwinn Coppinger who lived on Delmar Avenue which crossed Confederate Avenue one block north of Big Mama's house. She is my first cousin and the second grandchild of Big Mama and Big Daddy. I asked her to contribute this story as she lived so close for so long that she is much more familiar with the neighborhood and life from day to day at Big Mama's house during the 1940-1960 decades. She attended the Confederate Avenue Baptist Church, Roosevelt High School, and was married at Confederate Avenue Baptist to James Coppinger in 1959. On my visits during the summers and on holiday weekends, Brenda was always present and a significant part of my childhood years in Atlanta.

> *{Dear Jack, I hope this is the type of information you are seeking for your story. If not or you need additional just let me know.*
>
> *Reflecting on Big Mama's house and the old neighborhood these words come to mind, love, family and safety. We lived in a "Mayberryish" community even with the close proximity to the big city of Atlanta. The neighborhood was multigenerational with children remaining or returning upon adulthood. There were many other family ties as well.*
>
> *Big Daddy's cousin, Era Hughes Whitener lived on Delmar near Smithloff's grocery store and the Dooley family had once lived on Confederate Ave. at Atlanta Ave. right*

across the street from the Dixie Marble Co. where Big Daddy, Uncle Jack and even my Mother had worked at one time. We were close enough and safe enough to walk to school, Church, the pharmacy, and even Grant Park Zoo and the Cyclorama. If something was further away there was easy access to the bus as it made stops on Confederate Avenue. This was a definite convenience as most of the mothers and grandmothers did not drive a car.

Big Mama's house sat on a hill with wide, ascending flagstone steps and rock gardens on each side. This was abloom most of the year with white candy tuft and purple/blue ageratum. Each spring everything received a fresh coat of paint whether or not it was needed, and I was sent to the pharmacy for a "spring tonic" which consisted of cherry cola with cod liver oil! Big Mama called ahead and made the arrangements. Her home was always warm and welcoming with the world's most mouth watering smells emanating from the kitchen. Sally, (our Negro maid and loved member of the family), was there most of the time, an integral part of our lives. She loved us all and to her we were her "Cherens".

I remember the porch on the side of the house with the wringer washing machine and a view of the lovely garden of flowers and tomato plants outlined with large stones. There were fresh, cut flowers almost always in the house. Saturday afternoons Big Mama and our next door neighbor, Mrs. Geraldine (J. L.) Benton (always Bennie to me) would walk to the CAB church with flowers in hand and arrange them on the altar for Sunday services. The Benton's had a very large garden in the back of their house and provided the flowers.

Along the low, partial fence between Big Mama's house and Mrs. Sear's back yard there were grape vines growing and pomegranate bushes just in front of the fence.

Big Daddy built a play house in the back yard adjacent to the barn (this was before Big Mama accidentally burned the barn down, of course!), a swing set and a fish pond for all of the grandchildren to enjoy. When the fish died we were allowed to cool off in the pond as a respite to the sweltering summer heat. When we all grew up, new fish were added.

Beneath the large tree in the back yard there was a bench on which Big Daddy churned delicious homemade ice cream or cut into a watermelon which had been iced down in a large, silver, galvanized wash tub to the delight and enjoyment of all.

Excitement was in the air at Holiday times and on special occasions when everyone came for celebrations and delicious foods to be eaten on the large screened-in porch which ran the length of the back of the house. I remember the cool floors tiled in a mosaic pattern *with pieces of marble and granite provided by Big Daddy. Many happy times were had by all of us grandchildren on that porch playing board games and cards or just rocking on the glider. I remember a summer learning to play Canasta with you Jack, Peggy Leonard, and Marge Hosleton (sp?) who lived next door .Remembrance brings back days of innocence, joys, and sorrows but always love, abounding and abiding. How extremely lucky we were. Oh how I long for those good old days.}*

(Brenda Gwinn Coppinger)(2011)

More Stories from Brenda

{Jack, it is so good to hear from you. In answer to your questions regarding the old neighborhood, the name of the grocery store on Delmar between Confederate Avenue and Boulevard was called Smithloff's, and they lived on the premises. It was, as I recall, an old fashioned "general store" with meats, dairy, fresh produce and dry goods. They did in fact deliver to the home by a delivery boy on a bicycle. We could walk to the store by going up the alley to the street above Big Mama's house and then over to Delmar. There was another store in the opposite direction towards the Old Soldiers Home which was for the surviving Confederate War Soldiers. This was located near the end of Confederate Ave. and too far to walk. There was a trolley car that went to the Home. The rail lines, as I remember, ran from downtown (on Moreland Ave. or Memorial Dr.?) to the Home. You could visit there but I do not remember ever going into the buildings. Ironically I have recently seen a program on cable TV where they are restoring the neighborhoods off of Confederate Ave. and they are using the trolley car symbols as a motif on the street signs, mail boxes. Etc. It seems young families are moving into the area and restoring the homes because of the convenience and close proximity to downtown Atlanta.

Big Mama's next door neighbor was Mrs. Sears, the mother of Helen, Frank and W. B. Helen moved to Franklin, TN and was a realtor until her death. W.B. always loved Billie and wanted her to marry him. They were lifelong friends. He and his wife even visited her after she moved here to Florida. He moved to Canada and became a multimillionaire in the textile industry, I believe. I do not know what happened to Frank, but he might have been killed in WW2. The house on the opposite side of Big Mama was originally owned by John Evans, her brother. Following his death and after her remarriage Hortense and Roy Leonard (Peggy's father) lived there (along with Faye and John Jr.) Then they sold the house and moved several doors down the street. I do not know who the new owners were.

Keep in touch. Love, Brenda

Jack, after sending this I remembered there was a Homer Sears, too. I might be confused regarding Frank, unless perhaps he was the father of the family (for some reason I remember the name). However, I do recall Homer living there so that he was not killed during World War II. I realize this is not important but wanted to be as accurate as possible for a little old lady!!! Love, B (2011).}

Fig.27 Brenda Gwinn Coppinger

- See Appendix XIII for Nan Eaton's story of her Big Mama

Virgil (Our "Big Daddy") and our ("Big Mama") George never learned to drive a car. The family owned automobiles from time to time with their son Jack driving them as needed and desired. Their daughter Sue Gwinn also declined to learn to drive. The trolley and then the bus on Confederate Avenue supplied their needs for transportation along with family members available to take them along. The family attended the Confederate avenue Baptist Church about two long blocks up Confederate Avenue. Virgil was a Deacon and instrumental in the design and building of a new church sanctuary.

His workplace was in the opposite direction down Confederate Avenue towards the Confederate Soldier's Home at 890 Confederate Avenue., S.E., Atlanta, Ga. This was called The Dixie Marble & Granite Company. It is my understanding that this was owned by B. F. Coggins who owned The Berkley Granite Company. Virgil was the General Superintendent of Berkley Granite. Berkley made high quality memorials at this plant. They used granite from the B.F. Coggins deposit, the Piedmont

Quarry at Carlton Ga, a few miles west of Elberton, GA. The Corporation sold memorials throughout the United States. It is my recollection that my Dad worked there for some time before moving to Winnsboro SC. Mr. Coggins was a successful business man and held Virgil and Jack in respect. Letters in my records describe the business of Doberman Pincers which Dad kept and showed at dog shows for Mr. Coggins. Prinz Peter II was one of their prize dogs. This was in 1930.

OFFICE OF
B.F. COGGINS
CANDLER BLDG.
ATLANTA, GA.
September 25, 193

Mr. Jack Butterworth,
898 Confederate Ave.,
Atlanta, Ga.

I suggest that some Saturday afternoon

you carry your puppies out to Mr. L. F. Schelver

who lives out on Roswell Road about 4 miles from Buckhead. You will see a big sign with the name of John J". Woodside and on another sign you will see Mr.Schelver's name advertising his Dog Kennel, and I amsure you will have no trouble locating him.

Try and make him a proposition of $1.50 a piece for trimming their ears as I believe he will do it for that, but it might be better for you to wait until they get two or three weeks older. After you have had him do the work let me know and I will pay you the. amount you payout.

I amsending Dr. Hopping a check today for trimming the tails which I think is all out of reason, I am,

Very truly yours,

~-~~~~

B. F. COGGINS.

61

In 1937 there was difficulty with union workers in the Atlanta Memorial business. That was the impetus for the family moving to Winnsboro, S.C. Mr. Coggins was involved in trying to ride out the problem and the government's role with labor.

Mr. Virgil Butterworth

Supt. of Berkeley Granite Corp. Atlanta, Georgia

For the last several months I know you have been harassed, and worried to such a degree it was hard to accomplish anything.

I don't want any of us to lose the idea we are going to surrender our rights to any union man, non-union man or any group of men. We are going to run our business as we have always run it, and if a man lies down on the job, keep a record of his activities and if he is not doing his work satisfactory, there is always a chance to get rid of him and get a better man.

You have done some awfully good work, and I am not at all satisfied with the outcome of this thing, but the position the Government takes, there was nothing else for us to do but try to get the men back to work.

Let's all put our shoulders to the wheel and try and go somewhere.

(Letter from B.F. Coggins to Virgil Butterworth)

Big Daddy was a quiet man and a loyal husband, father, grandfather, and Churchman. He was a member of the Blue Lodge Masonic Order and was respected by his employer and employees. He retired eight years before his death. Near the end of his life he suffered from pulmonary difficulties. He worsened and was admitted to Emory Hospital in Decatur, Ga. He died there on 2 April, 1955. His life was difficult from the beginning but he raised a great family and grew a wonderful legacy for his family with his professional contributions, honesty, faithfulness, and belief in God. He is buried in Westview Cemetery, Atlanta, GA.

Fig.28 Virgil Ralph Butterworth

Superintendent Berkley Granite Corporation

Smithloff's Grocery, as Brenda mentioned, was within walking distance for Big Mama on Delmar Street. They also delivered from a phone call or note list order to the house by way of the "back alley". Most of the family friends lived within walking distance of their home. All essential needs were close to home. Life circled around family, home, and Church along Confederate Avenue.

Big Mama attended Reinhardt College in Waleska Georgia as a young lady. She continued to encourage education for her children and grandchildren

Fig.29 Reinhardt College Dormitory 1910-1933

Fig.30   Reinhardt College 1910-1913

Fig.31   George Wilberth Evans as a teenager in Canton, Ga.

Big Mama grew into a proud lady and a loving caregiver of her family and household. She commanded respect from all who knew her and was a fine example of the Southern Christian Lady. She worked hard for the Women's Missionary Union of the Confederate Baptist Church and the local Baptist organizations. She was on theAuxiliary Board of the Georgia Baptist Hospital in Atlanta for many years. She moved to Winnsboro with her daughters Billie, Mary, son Jack, daughter –in-Law Gertrude, and husband Virgil for a short time in 1935 and then returned to her beloved Atlanta. She lived there until major social changes occurred in her neighborhood in the 1970s. She then moved to Mansfield, GA to be near her daughter "Billy Campbell" and later Mary Turner. There she had her own home, a small cottage just suited for her lifestyle. Therefore for all her life she was surrounded by family and continued a love and tradition of family members offering full and continued support. She attended family reunions and encouraged others to attend. She enjoyed many trips to Pawley's Island and Litchfield with family, all the while reading her bible and 'holding court".

Fig.32 Fred and Mary Turner   *Fig.33 Sue and Buford (Bud) Gwinn*

Pawley's Island, South Carolina

Fig.34 Buford-Jack-Fred, Virgil in background
reenacting a Minstrel at a reunion

Buford Gwinn, Jack Butterworth, Fred Turner

Big Mama enjoyed games and spent much time playing them with her grandchildren. In Atlanta she provided many a trip downtown on the electric trolley and the bus. She knew how to entertain a boy in the big city and show him the points of interest. The center of interest to me as a boy was her "back yard" with the fish pond. She had goldfish swimming there much of the time. I played there with a boat I found on one of our "downtown" trips. It was metal and had a compartment for a candle. By heating a circle of tubes in the housing, it boiled water out the stern and drove the boat forward with a "putting" sound. This was good for many hours of play. She and big daddy had chickens in the far back yard and they were interesting to visit since we did not have them at home. Cousins Brenda, Peggy Leonard, and Faye Evans were usually around Big Mama and provided much socialization. They were both cousins and friends. Sue and Bud lived up Delmar and many days I visited with them and Brenda.

Big Mama was a member of The Baptist Camp just outside of Atlanta. She recruited my brother Jim Butterworth for a summer job at the site and he was worked very hard that "vacation". She reportedly played the guitar as a young girl but she abandoned that in later years. She loved music and surprisingly was a devout fan of Elvis Presley, especially his gospel songs. She abhorred the use of alcohol and counseled all in the ravages of its use. She went to Pawley's Island with my family in the late 1970s. I remember her sitting with Bible in lap and her watchful eyes on the children.

Near the end of life she developed symptoms related to carotid artery occlusion. At that time the surgery was considered risky and I asked her to suffer the dizziness and the sensation of fainting rather than undergo surgery. She wanted surgery however and I located a friend who was an Atlanta vascular surgeon. He performed surgery at the DeKalb Hospital but she succumbed during the post operative period. I believe she was fully prepared for her departure at age 89 years. She had lived a long and full Christian life. She left a great vacuum and many grandchildren who continue to have her influence in their lives. She is buried with her beloved husband Virgil in Westview Cemetery, Atlanta, GA.

Big Mama Stories from (Cousin) Brenda Gwinn Coppinger

{Jack, How exciting to have this additional information about our family. It fascinates me and I am anxious to learn more. I have heard Big Mama talk about living with her mother-in-law after she was married (at the age of 16? she really did not want us to know how young she was) and how much she learned from her (Sarilda Ann Hughes).

One of the stories I recall which always made Big Mama laugh when she told it was her first attempt at laundry. Being a new bride she wanted to do Big Daddy's shirts "to perfection" and insisted on doing them on her own without any assistance from her mother-in-law. Having no idea how much starch to put into the water she poured in the whole box and hung the shirts out to dry. When Big Daddy came home from work and tried to duck under the clothes line he pushed the shirts aside and they came back and hit him almost knocking him out because they were "as stiff as a board" with all of that starch.

I believe, if memory serves at this "advanced" age, there was a woman that worked for her father; she called her "Aunt Nancy" who was an influence on her life. She once related a story about taking one of her brothers "trousers", putting them on and riding a horse from her father's stable, astride not side saddle as a lady would, through town to the horror and embarrassment of Aunt Nancy.

I only know the story of James Henry Butterworth dying of pneumonia after helping people cross the river in his boat. Following his death Big Daddy did support his mother and brothers and sisters and they all lived together. I know nothing of the Fowlers except for Earl, Owen and Dean and some of the younger generation (about our ages)- Betty and Bobby-who came to visit Big Mama several times when I was growing up. I believe they lived somewhere in South Carolina. Mother told stories of Big Daddy at one time working for the railroad. Could this be when he was the steam engine mechanic?

They all lived together with GW Evans on Crew Street in Atlanta in a large home which he provided. Aunt Naomi was a widow by that time and she and Evans, Buena and Ralph lived with them as well. Mother told many stories of them playing as children.

She also had fond memories of Aunt Milan and Uncle Jim who lived close by. (Milam and Naomi were sisters to Big Mama) She said that Aunt Milan was such a sweet person and a good cook

Part II

Newby family

The maternal side of our family is one filled with interesting persons and a variety of geographical origins. The Newby family itself hails from England. A report compiled by the Roots Research Bureau, Ltd. states that the name of Newby was originally derived from the residence of its first bearers at Newby, a township in the union of Ripon, in Yorkshire, England. While there have been various spellings, the most recent in America is Newby as we know it. The family name has been found back to the 13th Century. John Newby, a Quaker, who hailed from County Westmoreland, England, was the progenitor of the Newbys of North Carolina. They lived in Pasquotank County, N.C. in the last half of the 17th cn. Newbys are prominent in the Isle of Wight and Nansemond Counties Virginia as well as in Pasquotank and Perquimans Counties North Carolina. These Virginia territories were populated by Church of England settlers. They did not tolerate the irascible Quakers who were opposed to taxation, military duty, and general incorporation into civil activities. Therefore Quakers migrated to more unsettled regions early.   Although we cannot definitely identify the Georgia Newbys to a specific site in North Carolina, we do have census reports stating that our oldest ancestor in Georgia was born in North Carolina as was his wife and other family members. Therefore we can reasonably identify our family as coming from the most prominent site of Newbys in that State. The first we find is in the area of the Isle of Wight Virginia. Then they moved just over the border into North Carolina along the coastal region. These families were Quakers so they had good records from the Meetings unless the houses were burned or a member was dismissed from the Meeting. It was not difficult to be dismissed from the Meeting as public service, to include military, dating a non Quaker, or even participating in horseracing would accomplish that dismissal.

Another family branch can be traced to Highland Scots who were recruited from the Inverness area in Highland Scotland to Georgia. General Oglethorpe invited Highlanders to settle the territory south of Savannah and to deal with the Spanish and Indians along the Florida border. The leader of this Highland Clan was Sixth Great Grandfather**John Mohr McIntosh.** His line dates to the MacIntoshes of Borlum who were active in the Jacobite rebellion in 1715. We are descended from Mary Ann McIntosh, John Mohr McIntosh's daughter. She married John Baillie also from Scotland. John remained a Tory during the Revolutionary War while her brothers, Lachlan and John, were prominent military leaders for the Revolutionaries. The story told is that the families remained close and friendly despite the differing political views in wartime. This line has been traced to Lachlan Badenoch McIntosh of Inverness-shire born n 1430.

The French Huguenot family of **Andre Rembert** immigrated to Charleston SC after the revocation of the Edict of Nantes in 1685. Louis XIV, the grandson of Henry IV, renounced the Edict and declared Protestantism illegal with the Edict of Fontainebleau. The Remberts left France and settled along the coast outside Charles Town before moving into upland South Carolina as farmers. This family can be traced back to their picturesque region of southern France, Pont en Royans. Loam Brown was the father of Mary Jane Brown my 2nd Great Grandmother. Loam's mother was Mary Polly Rembert, our 4th Great Grandmother. Her father was Abijah Rembert who descends from Andre Rembert the immigrant. Andre is my 8th Great Grandfather. This line has been traced to 1575 in France.

The **Key family** is one of importance in Virginia and South Carolina. We have traced this line to 1310 AD. There is a relationship with Francis Scott Key who wrote the "Star Spangled Banner". Tandy Clarke Key, fifth great grandfather, served in constructing forts along the Indian border of Georgia under Elijah Clark. Tandy was a Major and Comdt. of the 25th Reg., Georgia Militia. His orders instructed the building of the road to "Standing Peachtree and Fort Peachtree built by Nathaniel Garrison in Hall County during the War of 1812. The Key family has been traced to Richard Key of England born in 1310.

The **Harvey** and **Paulette** families are related to us and will need more work to flesh out their stories.

Knowing that we have named ancestors and families which relate to historical occasions makes an intriguing study in my mind. Our family is fortunate to have names and relationships to accompany European history and the causes for immigration to the new land of America. The formation and growth of our nation is readily seen through the progression of our ancestors who passed their heritage to us today.

Walden Family

Viola Paulette Walden married William Franklin Newby and is my Grandmother. Her family name also came from an English place name. Various spellings are listed in the Doomsday book and later. It is of the same derivation as the name for Wales. Our line has been traced to Samuel Walden born 1748 in South Carolina. The Walden Y DNA project links this Samuel Walden to the Samuel Walden/ Mary Dismukes of Halifax County, Virginia who is believed to descend from Lord John Walden of Ravensworth Castle in England. Another close link is to James Walden/Hannah Hatch of Vermont/ New York and to Henry Walden of Spartanburg, South Carolina. Research however, has not uncovered the direct connection to any of these families, nor to many of the subjects included as "matches" to this Samuel Walden.

Our Walden family moved to Jefferson County Georgia near present day Waynesboro, Georgia. The Walden family owned land in several counties because the names of the counties kept changing. The family and land never moved or changed. Hardy Sylvester Walden married Waltie Paulette Davies beginning our current line. Viola's sister, Clara, married a Peters who died young. She remarried a Clary who also died leaving her to raise a large family. We knew Clell, Murphy, and Ellis Clary who grew up in Valdosta. Ellis was a professional baseball player for the Atlanta Crackers and then the big leagues for many years. He later was a scout and recruiter for the Toronto Blue Jays until retirement. He operated the "Sportsman's Club" in Valdosta and was quite a well known sportsman of his time.

Exum Newby ca. 1786- 1875+

Exum was the name of my 3rd great-grandfather Newby. It has been spelled Axiom as well as other phonetic variations in various documents. We know from the 1830 census that **Exum** Newby was living then with his wife **Michele** in the part of Wilkerson County which later became Twiggs County, Georgia. They both stated their birthplace was in N.C. but no more details were required. Where Exum was born and what he did from birth to 1830 is not known. As a Quaker, several options come to mind. If he married outside the Meeting, he would have been expelled. If he joined the militia he also would not be accepted as a member. We do know that he left North Carolina which probably was the coastal region of Perquimans County and settled in the frontier of Georgia. Mr. Raymond Winslow of Hertford North Carolina performed a search for Exum Newby in the 1990s. Raymond was related to the Newby family of the area and did find several named men Exum, but not one of our birth date or migration record.

A land lottery was initiated in 1803 in Middle Georgia. This began in the area around Ft. Wilkerson and drew settlers into former Indian Territory of the Creek Indians. This lottery encouraged settlement and subsequent immigration to the area. There was good climate, abundant water, game, and fertile soil to be found. Historians have claimed that "hardly a descendant of any pioneer of the county but can claim descent from these Carolina settlers". The Carolinas furnished the majority but Virginia was well represented in this immigrant group of the early 19th century.

Exum Newby does not appear in the 1818 Twiggs County, Georgia Tax Digest which had been preserved, but Axiom Newby is listed in the 1826 Tax Roll, Twiggs County. He could have lived in Wilkinson County from which Twiggs was created prior to that time but the records are no longer available. Exum was noted to be able to read but not write and his name appears spelled in various fashions-Axiom, Exuum, Axum, and Exum. In the more complete 1850 census, A. Newby of the same age and family size owned 200 acres of land. Michele Hasty Newby is included in the 1850 listing along with Robert as a 19 year old male. We can conclude that Exum settled in Wilkinson-Twiggs County Georgia earlier than 1926, acquired land, and began his family with Michele, his North Carolina wife. She died between the 1860 and 1870 census recordings.

Hilliard Sylvester Newby 1819-1890

Hilliard Sylvester Newby, my great, great, grandfather was one of Exum's sons and is the ancestor Jim Butterworth and I used to join the Sons of Confederate Veterans. He is listed in the 1850 census as a farmer 31 years old in Twiggs County GA. His wife is named Mary Jane Grey and is 28 years old. We have no stories of this family but only records showing four children in 1850. Hilliard in 1860 is found to be living on a farm in Marion GA valued at $1450 with a total estate value of $1600. His wife, Mary Jane Grey has died by this time but left 6 children with Hilliard. The youngest named Hilliard Jr. is 7 years old. Hilliard must have been a responsible individual as he was named as administrator of the estate of Sarah Hasty who likely was sister of Michele Hasty Newby, his mother. Hilliard served as Postmaster of Twiggsville GA in March 27, 1888. Several Newbys held this same office.

There are many children in the household of Hilliard Newby over many years. These can be identified in the 1850-1870 census roles. After the death of his first wife, Hilliard married Sarah Newby. This added many changes to the family. She seems to have been a good business woman and family manager. She had three husbands to include Hilliard and thus many children. She would be a step grandmother to our line but is indeed an admirable character in many ways. She descended from the Foss and Andrews family of Maryland and Georgia. She was born in Houston Co and reared in Twiggs County. Her first husband, Wm. Hunter of Fort Valley died young and she married Bryant Asbell. She had six children with Hilliard and an estimate of over a dozen in total.

Hilliard joined the Army of the Confederacy and is found in the muster role of Company E, 63rd Regiment Georgia Volunteer Infantry C.S.A. Hilliard S. enlisted August 4 1863 at Savannah GA under Col. Harris for three years. He was sick in the Regimental hospital from Sept to Oct 1863 and was assigned as a nurse at the hospital in Nov and Dec 1863. He was present for muster in Jan and Feb.

Engagements of 63rd Infantry

- Battery Wagner, South Carolina (7/18/63)
- Atlanta Campaign, Georgia (5/64 - 9/64)
- Kennesaw Mountain, Georgia (6/27/64)
- Atlanta Siege, Georgia (7/64 - 9/64)
- Atlanta, Georgia (7/22/64)
- Jonesboro, Georgia (8/31/64 - 9/1/64)
- Franklin, Tennessee (11/30/64)
- Nashville, Tennessee (12/15/64 - 12/16/64)
- Carolinas Campaign (2/65 - 4/30/65)
- Bentonville, North Carolina (3/19/65 - 3/21/65)

Robert Ruffin Newby 1847-1xxx

Robert Ruffin was the son of Hilliard Sylvester Newby and my great-grandfather. Little is known of him at this time. He apparently was born in Twiggs County Ga as all of his relatives lived there. John H. Holliday researched Newby family history and found Robert in the Wilkinson County census in 1870. He was 33 years old and married to Elizabeth who was 24 years old. We have no record of Elizabeth's last name. His second wife was named Sally and the mother of additional children. He had two sons at the time of the 1870 census and the youngest was William F. Newby, my Grandfather. The families were large and sometimes the first wife died with the husband having subsequent children by a second wife. These families almost always lived on farms and the children were an asset in managing the crops. Robert had at least eight children who were siblings to our grandfather. Robert was too young for the War. He was noted to have 250 acres of land in Wilkinson County in 1870. The county was divided and the family farm was along the dividing line. Unfortunately that is all we know of Robert Ruffin. He was a farmer in Wilkinson County adjacent to other family farms in Twiggs County. He had a large family with two wives as mothers. He was the father of my grandfather William Franklin Newby. Robert Lee Newby, Jr. believed that Robert Ruffin financially helped his son William Franklin to start his first general store in Dooly County in the late 1800s.

William Franklin Newby 1870-1925

Fig.35 Viola Paulette Walden Newby   *Fig.36 William Franklin Newby*

Grandfather W.F. Newby was born on his father's farm in Wilkinson County Georgia in 1870. His mother was named Elizabeth. He had at least five brothers and one sister. William was the second born with James Ira a year older. The early years are not known or recorded. It is family lore that he did not like the farm life and once he left it he never desired to return. Although his son, Robert

Lee, owned farm land in Dooly County, William Franklin did not participate in the management or operation. His early education is not recorded but he must have learned his fundamentals early. He moved from Wilkinson County and married Viola Paulette Walden on 11 Oct., 1894 at the age of 24. They lived in a community in Dooly County called Richwood. It was a terminus of a working lumber railroad from 1897 to 1903. There was an opportunity for a mercantile business supplying that commercial activity. W.F. Newby's obituary says he originally worked for the Parrott Lumber Company in Richwood. The railroad was used to transport that lumber to market.

Dooly Southern Railway

The Dooly Southern received its charter on January 21, 1897 and completed its 9-mile line between Richwood and Pinia in August of 1898. It was operated by the Parrott Lumber Company but served as a common carrier as well as a logging road. One of its advertisements noted that it was "operated for freight business, but passengers are carried on freight trains." It was abandoned in early 1903.

The Georgia State Gazetteer of 1896 listed Penia as a place of 100 residents on the Savannah, Americus & Montgomery Railroad about five and one-half miles east of Cordele. Its businesses consisted mainly of sawmills and naval stores operations. Richwood, the community at the other end of the line, lies between Vienna and Cordele. It seems that lumber from the Richwood region was transported via the Dooly Southern to Penia and then to Savannah on the SA&M.

> **DOOLY SOUTHERN RAILWAY.**
> B. P. O'NEAL, President, Richwood, Ga.
> From **Richwood**[1] to Lath (1 mile), Dorough (4 miles) and **Penia**[2] (8 miles). Operated for freight business, but passengers are carried on freight trains. *August*, 1902.
> **Connections.**—[1] With Georgia Southern & Florida Ry. [2] With Seaboard Air Line Ry.

Richwood is located just outside of Vienna. It is close to the Shiloh Church where the Walden, Newby, and Brown family lived and attended church.

Fig.37 Shiloh Church, Dooly County, Georgia

William learned his trade well when with Parrott. Robert Newby Jr., a later owner and operator of Newby's Store, said in a news article that Robert Ruffin (Ruskin) Newby, W.F.'s father initiated the store as an experimental barometer. So that may have been the initial financing for the Newby Store in Vienna.

Fig.38 William F. And Viola Paulette Walden Newby Wedding Picture 1894

One can see that the detailed stories of our distant relatives are incomplete and the census recordsare required to know any information at all on occasions. Their daily lives are not recorded, leaving us with conjecture and extrapolation from other histories of the times. Undoubtedly they had the same trials and rewards we know today but in their own environmental capsule. At this juncture I wish to insert some of the family names and known stories before we get to the history of our current era family.

Our Grandmother **Viola Paulette Walden** has a rich family line that invites us to exciting areas. Some of this information has been stated already but bears reference at this point to show the lineage. Viola's maiden name of **Walden** is one we have traced back for five generations from Viola to Samuel Walden who was born in South Carolina in 1748 and moved to live in Warren and Jefferson County GA.

Fig.39 Walter (ie) Paulette Davies Walden-Viola's Mother

Fig.40 William Franklin and Viola Walden Newby

Her mother was a **Davies** and that family leads to the **Key** family of SC and VA., and the **McIntosh family** of Darien, McIntosh County, GA. These families, as noted, participated in the founding of the state of Georgia, the Revolutionary War, and War of 1812 where members can be found in both the Tory and the Colonialist armies. The family of **Loam Brown** is large and we are closely related through Viola's grandmother Mary Jane Brown (Davies) (Murray), who was a major influence in the lives of the Newby daughters of William and Viola. I have put the dates and names on theAncestry. com list under Butterworth/Evans: Newby/Walden Tree

Fig.41 Viola Paulette Walden Newby

Historic Home Of The Week

O.S. Bazemore reportedly built the Newby home at 415 Union St. in 1880 of selected heart pine with white oak roofing. He and his family lived in the dwelling until the early 1900's when W.F. Newby bought it. Present owners are Mr. and Mrs. J.F. Forbes (the former Alice Newby, a daughter of Mr. Newby.)

Unusual features of the house include a wide oak front door with stained glass, fireplaces with beveled glass mirrors and ornamental glazed tile facings. Stained wainscotting and wide-plank stained floors which were typical of the era in which the house was built are evident throughout.

Ceilings in the parlor, hall and dining room are of embossed terne metal and the walls are made of tongue and grooved wood papered on a cloth overlay which was also common in the late 1800's. Light fixtures are all tiffany style, and a storm pit is provided under the porch.

Shutters were on all the original windows and the back porch was latticed.

This home is just one of many in Vienna included in the Vienna Junior Woman's Club's walking/riding historic tour of homes. A brochure about the tour has been printed, and will be ready for distribution soon.

Fig.42 Burr's (Viola Newby) House on Union Street Vienna, Georgia

Fig.43 415 Union Street ca. 1900

If ever there was a homestead truly filled with stories and love, it would be exactly like this house. A son, five daughters, granddaughters, grandsons brothers, in-laws, great- grandparents, and friends found a warm and adventure filled atmosphere in this structure. Christmas celebrations, family dinners, daily life, sewing bees, and bandit break-ins provide the theme of a rich and full family life at this site.

W.F. Newby bought the Bazemore house at 415 Union Street, Vienna GA in the early 1900s. A large family was born, raised, and many died in this home. Daughter and Mother Gertrude said that many family members were "laid out" in the Parlor with all night vigils after their death. William Gladstone who died at an early age and Robert Lee were the sons. Audrey, Alice, Mary, Gertrude, Aurelia, and

Hilda Newby, who was born July 24, 1909 and died April 13, 1911, were the daughters. Viola was noted always to be sad in April because of the loss of her little girl.

The home on Union Street was known as Burr's house to most of us family. The large front porch of their house was a delightful spot for generations. Later it was "screened in" to keep out bugs. Dances and parties with increasing numbers of young men was a common occurrence. The "front parlor" was used for special occasions and was unique by having no communication with the rest of the house. It was heated only by a fireplace and quite cold on Christmas Mornings. A "wind up" Victrola was a feature of the Parlor. Mother said that cardboard records which sold for 5 cents were available weekly featuring the latest hits. Dancing was common on the porch and parlor. They had a piano and it was common for all young ladies to learn to play, and these did, performing for family members on their visits.

Underneath the front bedroom was a "storm cellar". Whether anyone ever occupied it during a storm is not known. However it was a frequent retreat for the young girls using their dolls to play housekeeping.

The house has a large elaborate front door of dark mahogany styled wood. At one time it had a bell in the center which remained but was not operative. The door opened into a foyer that ran to the dining room. Just inside the front door I remember well the wall telephone with a hand crank on the right side of the wooden box. There was a fixed mouthpiece and an earpiece on a long cord. One would wind the crank and the operator was summoned to the line. You then gave her the number and she connected you. She could listen to the conversation and was known to join the conversation if she had additional information to offer. I remember vividly because on summer vacations I got homesick at night and called home on that phone.

Immediately off to the right side was Burr's room with two double beds, rockers, a stove, and sewing machine. This was the central area of visiting for family and close friends Newby Kelt recalled when there was a single light hanging from the middle ceiling run in with external wiring. Electricity likely was added as it became available in Vienna. A pot for night time necessity was often used as the only bathroom was at the far end of the back porch. That was a cold walk indeed during winter.

If you turned left off the foyer you entered the "other room". This was the second bedroom and for many years the bedroom for Mary, Aunt Minnie Tharpe and her daughters Mary and Shirley. They lived with Burr for many years as the girls grew up in this house.

The dining room was a big one with a central table which hosted the large family. Sideboards lined the walls and were often loaded with holiday food and deserts. A single fireplace was adorned with tiles. This was not used as a fireplace but vented a stove from time to time. Off from the dining room was the sleeping porch. It was used by guests and Uncle Hardy from time to time. It was also cold on winter nights, but quilts made from wool suit samples fought the chill.

Fig.44 1940 Christmas Dinner at Burr's House

Buddy, Melissa, Sity, Newby, Robert Jr., Burr, Little Mary, Shirley, Minnie,
Mary Kelt, Bit, Kelly, Al, Joe Forbes

The back side of the dining room led into the large kitchen. There was also a side door leading to the long back porch.

The kitchen had electrical appliances but in addition had a wood stove which was used for heating as well as cooking. This area usually was occupied by a Negro cook who was picked up at home and often stayed the day to assist with the meals on holidays. Off of the kitchen was a closet for storage and hanging hams. It was known as "Hardy's Room" for many years. Burr's brother Hardy Sylvester Walden visited often and lived with Burr on occasion. He was well liked by the family and was a favorite of Burr who depended on Hardy for odd jobs and repair after the death of Mr. Newby. This area had an outside door which made it perfect for Hardy who kept his own hours. Uncle Hardy was an interesting person who never seemed to settle down in one place. He had served in the Marine Corps during WWI. It was told that he lost his wife or sweetheart as a young man and lamented her the remainder of life. When in Vienna he worked sometimes at the Newby store. He lived in Atlanta when Audrey was first married and apparently visited with relatives from time to time. It was said that Burr many times heard the train whistle down Union Street and would sit up in bed and say, there is the train, and Hardy's coming. And sure enough he soon would walk up on the porch. Maybe she had a special intuition.

Fig.45 Uncle Hardy Walden

{*Jack, I don't know the specifics you have asked. I know that Hardy served in the Military somewhere as he used the VA for various treatments, and ultimately died in a VA Hospital.*

I don't know where or when "Aurelia:"became his wife, nor what happened to her.

So put on your Sherlock Holmes Deerstalker Hat for the following:

My Father served in WW-1 and Uncle Hardy was truly many years older than my Father.

As a child, it was always understood that Uncle Hardy was a Veteran of the Spanish-American War…even as a Teddy Roosevelt "Rough Rider"…

Perhaps an old Veteran's well known improvement of their service, but perhaps not…

Murphy Clary believed it, and bailed him out of multiple scrapes in Macon, GA. Where Murphy was an up and coming lightweight boxer, and Hardy was a Famously Mean Drunk and was frequently jailed in Macon, waiting for Murphy to rescue him.

Once, Murphy said, to me and others, he got Hardy out of jail using Murphy's reputation as a Boxer and his "Good Will" account with the Sheriff and over the strong recommendation by the Sheriff that he not do it.

Hardy Walden was a very large, strong, man. Murphy Clary, though handy with his fists, was a much smaller specimen of the species.

As soon as they were clear of the Police Station and Jail, Uncle Hardy beat him up for having said that he helped him when he needed help.

In telling the story, Murphy said, "Next time, I just let him stay long enough to sober-up like the Sheriff said I should have done the first time.

But that's another story isn't it? You need some of Murphy's boys for that one.

Uncle Hardy did build Liberty Ships in Jacksonville during WW 11.

Not related to your question but, after all, you started this...

Uncle Hardy was not an educated man. But he has several "saying" he was fond of repeating.:

I am reasonably sure that none of them were original with him, but he liked them and used them often when with me:

Fig.46 Lt. J.G. Robert Newby, Jr. and Hardy Walden

1. Never try to catch a falling knife.

2. Never play poker with a man named "Doc"

3. Never eat at a diner called "Moms"

4. Then when the appearance of something displeased him:

>   *"That looks worse than shit in the road!"*

Jack, if you don't want stuff like this, then don't ask, as it seems

That I can't control it once it starts.

Love to you and yours, Newby}

The kitchen led to the back porch on the East side of the house. This wonderful porch had two ice chests that were stocked with blocks of ice for refrigeration. It was screened and covered with a lattice work for shading. The house side of the porch was often filled with stacks of watermelons of different varieties in preparation for the arrival of guests which was us. A water board was on the outside wall and a faucet allowed washing with direct drainage to the outside. This was great for cleaning of fish and game and often used for that purpose. The rear of the porch led outside to steps to the yard. Adjacent to the rear door was a door to a long bathroom with a commode, sink, and claw foot bathtub. An electric heater tried to keep this area warm on cold days but struggled mightily without great success. This single bathroom was busy and some scheduling for bathing was necessary. The back yard of this house was large. Several pecan trees shaded the yard and kept grass from growing near the house. The sandy yard required broom sweeping from time to time to keep clean. The unpaved drive way allowed parking near the house and on holidays it was filled with family vehicles. At one time a barn was situated on a corner next the alley which ran from Union Street to Church Street. Mother said they had a cow when she was young but I only saw a large load of corn in the barn as evidence of practical use. Mary, Newby, and Shirley played in the barn as children. The far rear of the lot was plowed for a garden for many years. It was a large garden and tended by Burr herself, Hardy, and sometimes hired hands. It was mule plowed many years with corn, beans, tomatoes, and other vegetables harvested in the fall. Mother said they had "hog killing" in the fall and everyone pitched in to butcher the meat, make sausage, and render fat for lard and tallow in her childhood days. That was an important occasion for that season of the year and established the sayings of "hog killing time" or "cold enough to hang meat". Hardy's room usually had one or two hams hanging each winter. A small storage shed in the back yard also was a site for ham storage after curing. Usually the hams were salt cured but could be smoked or sugar cured.

Fig.47 *Family Christmas Portrait Burr's Parlor ca. 1954*

Back: Jimmy, Joe Forbes, Alice, Gert, Audrey Kelt, Mary Cobb, Jack Sr., Guy Cobb, (Guy T.)

Front- Mary Tharpe, Bill Henderson, Shirley Henderson, Melody Newby, Marie Newby, Robert Jr. with Bobbie

Jack and Audrey (Sity to us) purchased the house adjoining Burr's lot when Jack retired. They moved from Bayside, NY to Vienna. This was a convenient location and kept the family in close proximity.

For me Christmas vacation was a trip to Burr's house. Bit and Kelly Pharr and their sons came from Decatur Ga. The Vienna crowd of Burr, Al and Joe, Aunt Minnie, Mary and Shirley, Melissa, Marie, Robert Jr and his children Melody and Bobby were all part of the festivities. We enjoyed visiting at Forbes Drug Store and Newby's Store across the street. My Dad, Jack, knew many of the non-family men in town and had a great enjoyment with Robert and Joe and the locals. One of my memories is of the trips we made to the ice house to be sure we had adequate ice blocks for the meals. Kelly Pharr, Dad, Jack Kelt and I would ride to the ice house with me listening to the grownup conversation and humor. This same activity would occur on summer trips too. We stayed late down town on Christmas Eve and Summer Saturday nights. There always was a very large crowd in town and the streets were filled with people and cars. All the stores stayed open until 10 -11 PM. I was told that these were farmers who came to town on Saturday for shopping, but some of it was entertainment I am sure. We traveled from Marietta, Athens, and Gainesville GA to Vienna in cars with minimal heaters. We used blankets and comforters to brace the cold and thrilled at the town and home decorations as we traveled the four hours to Vienna. The four of us sang Christmas Carols and other songs with everyone joining in. Santa Clause came with us and for decades Jim and I either played the game or believed Santa knew where we could be located.

Part III

Gertrude Annette Newby 1911-2007

The early family life of the Newby family is largely an embellished memory based on speculation and knowledge of the times by reading and talking with older individuals. The later years are enriched by my Mother, Gertrude who was great to relate stories of her childhood giving us a very true history.

Gertrude attended Grammar school in Vienna, Georgia. There was only one school for town children, except for Negro children. All grades were held in one schoolhouse.

Fig.48 2ⁿᵈ Grade VHS 1919

Her sixth grade memo book contains a letter from Miss Blalock her teacher who was from Valdosta. It is a thank you for an end of school gift and expresses her enjoyment of having her in her class. Miss Wells also sent her a letter from Rochelle, GA on August 16, 1922. This one spoke of the affection she held for Gertrude and other boys and girls n her class. She said" I'm counting on you to be the same smart little girl for Miss Clara Mae that you were for me." With assurance that Gertrude had a nice time while at the Camp Ground, she gave her love and anticipation to see her again "before long". These letters convey the sense of a close knit small town relationship of an enjoyable childhood. Cut-out souvenirs from the Krazy Klub show the fun social side of her school years. The memo book labeled sixth grade contains clippings from the seventh and eighth grade as well as a graduation picture from High School. At the Jr/Sr Banquet the eighth grade served the others with Napkins, Paper Flowers, and a small Paper Parasol. - A high time indeed!

Fig.49 Quinnie Carmack and Gertrude Newby High School Seniors

One of her best friends was Quinnie Carmack. They socialized at an early age and Mother remembered their friendship all of her life. This notice in the Vienna News society column verifies one occasion.

Mother saved her school records and papers. She was awarded honor status on many occasions. She had older and younger sisters in school at the same time and one can imagine the activity on Union Street. Viola and later her daughters themselves made most of the clothes for the girls. I was told that the girls with their Mother selected patterns and fabric at the Newby store and had new outfits for each season.

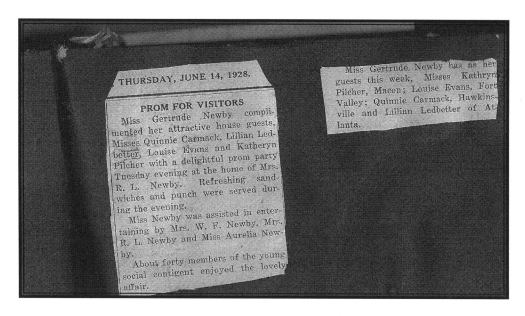

Fig.50 Vienna Society News

Fig.51 "To the Beach"

Fig.52 Aurelia (Bit) and Gertrude

Georgia State Normal School-Athens, Georgia

Following High School graduation, Gertrude decided to follow her sisters into a career in Teaching. She attended Mercer College in Macon for a semester and then the Georgia State Teacher's College for Women in Athens, Ga. This was a two year school called The Normal School and was located at the end of Prince Avenue in Normal Town. There she studied an array of courses from English to Elementary Education and Physical Education. It served as a finishing school for most of the girls. Gert made many friends, sang in the Glee Club, and socialized in her Sorority. One of her roommates was Rosalyn Braselton from Braselton, GA. Her family owned the large General store of the area.

Fig.53 Winnie Davis Hall Georgia State Normal School

Newby Kelt said that the school was called Normal School because there were a fixed number of teachers in the State and that was the Normal. When one retired or resigned, another was placed, thereby restoring Normal. While attending school, there were no Co-EDs at the University of Georgia. They "integrated" the year she graduated. Gertrude said she was among the first females to attend a football game at the University. It must have been dull to go to games before that paradigm change.

Fig.54 *Gertrude Newby*

Burr's house and the Newby family hosted the occasion of the wedding of Jack Butterworth and Gertrude Newby on 14 Apr, 1934. The house had been the wedding site for other daughters and once again was a festive place. All the cousins and sisters with their husbands and beaus were in the party. I was told many times how Robert Jr., an adolescent at the time, bombarded my Dad with Cherry Bombs on his first visit to Vienna and Burr's house. Robert was always a fan on fireworks and this delighted my sons in later years. The Vienna Methodist Church provided the official sanctity of the day

Fig.55 Gertrude's Wedding Day

Jack met Gertrude while she lived with Sister Audrey and her husband Jack Kelt in their home in Decatur, Ga. Gertrude operated a kindergarten in the house at the time.

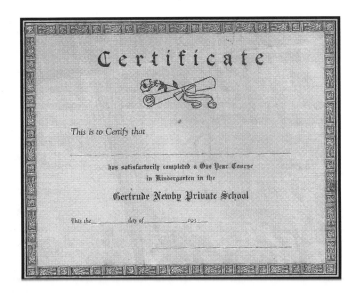

Fig.56 Graduation Certificate from Gertrude's Kindergarten in Decatur, GA

Fig.57 Leaving for Honeymoon

After an Atlanta courtship and visiting with Jack's sisters, Sue Gwinn, Mary Turner, and Billy Butterworth, the marriage was complete. They honeymooned in Charleston, SC and shortly moved with the Butterworth family to Winnsboro, SC.

Virgil had been employed in the Marble and Granite business in Atlanta but "union problems" began and he ventured to Winnsboro in the same line of work. Jack went with him as did daughter Billie who was in High School. Mary and Fred Turner lived there as Fred was originally from the town.

Gert and Jack moved into the Du Bose home in Winnsboro. They had an upstairs apartment. This is a picture of Gert waving from her apartment to Jack as he left for work.

Fig.58 First Home

On July 1, 1936 the couple moved to Mrs. Eugenia McMaster's house and bought their first bedroom suit. They were still in an upstairs apartment. On their first wedding anniversary they visited Washington D.C. and stayed at the Mimsly Hotel in Luray VA and the Hotel Commodore at Union Station in Capitol Plaza in Washington. For their gift they bought a G.E. Refrigerator –"Just What I Wanted!"

We have many letters from Winnsboro where Gertrude began her married life and communicated with her sisters and mother in Georgia. Jack opened the Butterworth & Neal operation as Granite Manufacturers in Winnsboro. Their logo showed "Mt. Zion Blue and Carolina Pearl, Wholesale". W.W. Neal and J.E. Butterworth were the principals. This company closed after two years.

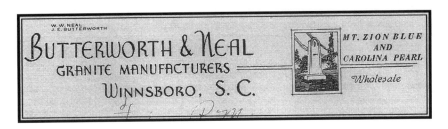

During that stay of three or four years, Jack enjoyed golf at the Country Club which was located on the edge of town where he also played tennis quite well with friends. In December of 1937 Jack Jr. was born in Mrs. McMaster's house on Main Street of Winnsboro. Dr. Buchanan was his delivering physician, at home.

Fig.59 Jackie and Gert 1937

Jackson Evans Butterworth, Sr. 1908-1989

My Dad was Jackson Evans Butterworth. He was named for Uncle Andrew Jackson Evans, his mother's brother. In the time period of 1900's it was common to name babies, in the South at least, after Presidents or heroic characters. Andrew Jackson had been a hero and a President some years before Andrew Jackson Evans' birth. He may have been quite important to citizens of Cherokee County, Ga. since he was instrumental, and brutal, in moving the Indians out of the region in 1838. So this naming of Jackson Evans Butterworth kept a family tradition alive as well as retaining a memory of a departed relative.

Early in Jack's life, as previously noted, Virgil, George, and Jack moved to live with Emma Fowler, Virgil's sister. This was close to the home of Sarilda Hughes Butterworth who was a widow at the time. Jack was fond of the Fowlers all his life although there was little interaction in later years. The family lived in Canton until Jack was about 10 years old. He never shared any information about his life in Canton other than he enjoyed visiting on the Sutalle farm of Uncle Henry and riding horseback. This farm was only 10 miles or so from town but I imagine it seems like a trip to the country for him. The farm was part of the large land holdings of the Knox and Evans family on the road to Waleska.

Jack lived a short time on Crew Street and when I visited there he reflected on his living there. I do think he had fond memories of living at Delta Place next door to his double first cousin John Evans Butterworth and the Mills family. He had an abundance of Aunts around as well as cousins. During his teen age years and as a young man he lived at 847 Confederate Avenue. Big Mama told us of his playing basketball with a City Team and her concern that he was "injuring his health" by excessive activity.

Fig.60 Jack and Moorland Basketball Team

He did contract pneumonia which was a feared illness of the time. He said he was cured of "double pneumonia" by a "lady" doctor who he held in high regard. This time period was before the advent of antibiotics, even sulfa. Pneumonia was fatal to persons burdened with other physical conditions.

Fig.61   Jack Evans Butterworth Elementary School ca 1919

He also developed musical skills. He played saxophone and clarinet in a band he organized. The band played in prominent sites and he told me of playing jobs at the Blue Room in the Biltmore Hotel. This was a significant achievement for his age group. He related a story of how one night the group was playing at the Biltmore and someone asked him if a visitor could sit in and play his saxophone for a tune. Jack agreed and the player, a professional musician, played so well that Jack felt "upstaged" for the remainder of the evening. He said he learned not to lend his horn out during a gig from then forward. Dad repeatedly asked me if I had ever heard of Rudy Weidoeft, a saxophone player. But I had never heard of the artist. I did ask several woodwind men but never got a glimmer of recognition of the name. I concluded that Dad had misremembered the name. Several years after Dad's death I visited the music room in Thomas Edison's lab in West Orange, NJ. The park ranger asked if I would like to hear one of the early disc recordings on the Edison machine and I said yes of course. He played a tune with a saxophonist exhibiting great dexterity and range. I looked at the label and it was Rudy Weidoeft! Later I did more research and found that Rudy was imitated by many artists of his time and considered a pioneer of the saxophone style of the 20s and 30s. Dad was on target again and the modern musicians had forgotten Rudy and even how to spell his name.

Rudy Weidoeft in 1919, playing a <u>BuescherC melody saxophone</u>

Fig.62 *Rudy Weidoeft in 1919 playing a Buescher C melody saxophone*

Jack Attended Tech High School in Atlanta. He took great pride in his school and the "Tech Boys" felt <u>manly</u> compared to the Boy's High school. The school had a high military leaning and the yearbook shows the classes in military uniforms with the high boots of <u>WWI</u> style. The training was more technical than liberal arts, having an engineering bent. This pushed Dad into design and construction for his later profession. The school began, therefore, as an institution for white males, divided into Boys High School and Tech High. Because Boys High and Tech High were the only high schools for white males in early twentieth century Atlanta, these schools count among their graduates many of Atlanta's most influential citizens in the past fifty years. One of Jack's distant cousins graduated from Boy's High the same year he did. His name was Dean Rusk, also from Cherokee County Georgia. He later rose to prominence as Secretary of State under President John Kennedy and Lyndon Johnson.

Ennisville, THS:

Ennisville has had a most successful year, going over the top in all school activities. This class has supported all minstrel and dramatic club plays, and all football games, to the last man.

Under the teaching of our mayor, Mr. E. P. Ennis, we have learned much of the advanced English Literature of English 8.

Ennisville produced many of the most famous citizens of the United States of Tech High: Glenn Holland, our football captain and president of the Senior Class; Bob Randolph, all-state fullback; "Track Man" Ferger, a star of the track team; and the military officers, Holmes, Morton, Mitchell, Embry, and Cogbill. We had one Honor Roll man, Lane Mitchell, Jr., our class leader.

Our city directory shows that the following are citizens of Ennisville:

CLASS ROLL

Bacon, P. B.	Hill, M. T.	Randolph, Bob
Bowie, W. V.	Holland, Glenn	Scott, H. M.
Butterworth, Jack	Holmes, A. M.	Sewell, C. M.
Carnes, R. E.	Miller, M. H.	Stringer, J. F.
Cogbill, D. O., Jr.	Mitchell, Lane, Jr.	Stringer, W. K.
Embrey, J. T.	Mann, G. M.	Warren, J. C.
Ferger, Ed	Marsh, C. E.	Whigham, S. J.
Hendley, J. M.	Morton, Geo. L.	Whiteman, L.
	Whiteman, W. H.	

Fig.63 TEHISEAN

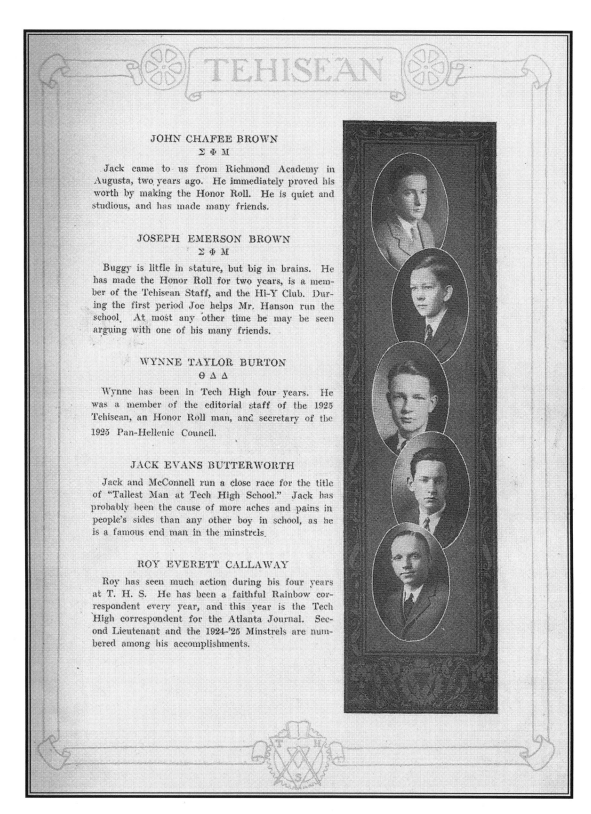

JOHN CHAFEE BROWN
Σ Φ M

Jack came to us from Richmond Academy in Augusta, two years ago. He immediately proved his worth by making the Honor Roll. He is quiet and studious, and has made many friends.

JOSEPH EMERSON BROWN
Σ Φ M

Buggy is little in stature, but big in brains. He has made the Honor Roll for two years, is a member of the Tehisean Staff, and the Hi-Y Club. During the first period Joe helps Mr. Hanson run the school. At most any other time he may be seen arguing with one of his many friends.

WYNNE TAYLOR BURTON
Θ Δ Δ

Wynne has been in Tech High four years. He was a member of the editorial staff of the 1925 Tehisean, an Honor Roll man, and secretary of the 1925 Pan-Hellenic Council.

JACK EVANS BUTTERWORTH

Jack and McConnell run a close race for the title of "Tallest Man at Tech High School." Jack has probably been the cause of more aches and pains in people's sides than any other boy in school, as he is a famous end man in the minstrels.

ROY EVERETT CALLAWAY

Roy has seen much action during his four years at T. H. S. He has been a faithful Rainbow correspondent every year, and this year is the Tech High correspondent for the Atlanta Journal. Second Lieutenant and the 1924-'25 Minstrels are numbered among his accomplishments.

Fig. 64 Tech High 1925

Fig. 65 Jackson Evans Butterworth 1927

The Tech High and Boy's High football games in the early 1900s drew crowds up to 20,000, more than Georgia or Tech College games. The series started in 1912 and ended with the restructuring of the city school system after the 1946 game. Tech High won the most games (18 to Boys' High's 15), including the finale played at Georgia Tech's Grant Field before one of the year's biggest crowds, 23,000. There was one tie in the series, 13-13, in 1944.

{*The biggest victory margin was in 1924 when Stumpy Thomason, who led Georgia Tech to a Rose Bowl victory in 1928, ran wild in a 69-0 Tech High rout. Boys' High's biggest victory margin came in 1941 when the immortal Clint Castleberry, the next year an All-American in his only season at Georgia Tech (he was killed in World War II) annihilated the Smithies, 45-0. The late Boys' High coach, R. L. (Shorty) Doyal, said of Castleberry, "He was so good I had to take him out of the games to hold the score down."*}

Imagine the intensity of the rivalry. The two schools were housed in the same building on Eighth Street stretching from Charles Allen Drive to Monroe Drive. In addition, each school had its own wooden portable stands, Boys' High on Charles Allen Drive and Tech High just around the corner on Monroe Drive.

The football teams practiced at the same time and at the same place - Piedmont Park. Boys' High had its field on the south end and just a few steps away Tech High worked out on the north end. You could say they were spittin' distance apart. The fields were on the west end of the Park, opposite 14th Street.

Jack was known to be a gifted artist during his early years. After High School he was offered an opportunity to study in New York City in 1939 with Mr. Boswick, a noted designer. He studied there for at least six months before returning to Atlanta and the design department of the Etowah Marble and Granite Company. The time from graduation and marriage was only 9 years. During this time he was a member of the Confederate Avenue Baptist Church and busily involved with basketball and music in addition to his work. Jack enjoyed automobiles and told of challenging his cars on the steep hill up Atlanta Avenue SE to Grant's Park. In October 12, 1927 Big Daddy, who did not drive purchased a used Buick sedan for the family at $ 1125.00. Jack was the likely driver. My Dad was the chief driver for his family before he was married. He told me they had several large cars to include a big Desoto. I think he had other cars while single. I know Mother's family had cars soon after they were available. My grandfather and grandmother Butterworth and Grandmother Newby and Aunt Sue Gwinn never learned to drive. Automobiles were never a high priority for Dad when I was in High School, just useful conveyance, until I was in College. This was a disappointment to me as a teenager of course.

Fig. 66 1924 Buick Roadster

Big Daddy purchased a Buick like this one in 1926. He did not drive.

Fig. 67 De Sota Six

Jack purchased a Desoto on 5 September 1931. His bill of purchase was for $558.00. This was quite a deal for a 23 year old young man.

Gert and Jack married in April 1934 and his story is intimately entwined with hers from that point forward. Jack and Gertrude married when he was 26 years of age in 1934.

Dad was extremely talented artistically, athletically, and mechanically. He spent much time showing me the auto mechanics necessary to keep a '41 Plymouth on the road. His design ability led him to worknot only in the Memorial Design business but as Manager of Gainesville Sheet Metal Company, Carroll Daniel Construction Design, and as a conceptual interior designer for businesses, homes, and Churches. The collection of his design blueprints and drawings have enthralled people all of his life. He was sought after for his talents from many directions and he "rendered' to them all, often without remuneration. He felt that people would pay him his due but learned that many tried to get away with no payment for "Drawing lines on paper". He never was driven by economic motives and enjoyed a quiet family life expecting that all would work out in God's time. This was a reproduction of his father's life-view and it did work out well for them both.

Part IV

Atlanta- the Return

Winnsboro was home for the Butterworth family for a few years. First Virgil and George, with Billie, returned to Atlanta in February of 1936 and moved to a rental house on Delmar Avenue in Atlanta. Their Confederate avenue house was rented and they had to wait before reclaiming it as home. On the family return to Atlanta they had difficulty with the car spinning in the road due to bad weather and ending up in a ditch. They had to get a farmer to pull them out with the help of two "northern men" who avoided the spinout because the Butterworth car was in the road. They arrived in Atlanta at 3:30 AM with no furniture in place -quite a "return of the natives". The Delmar house was large and rooms were available for Jack, Gert, and Jackie as they soon followed to Atlanta. Sue and Buford lived down the street so they were reunited with family. Buford operated a Shoe Repair shop on Lucky Street in downtown Atlanta at that time and until retirement. His mother and father lived one block off Confederate Avenue so they also were close by. The Butterworth family resumed worship at the Confederate Avenue Baptist Church and Virgil resumed work for Mr. Coggins at the Berkley Granite operation (Etowah Marble and Granite Company) on Confederate Avenue. Jack may have worked there for a time also. Jack received an opportunity with McNeil Marble and Granite in Marietta Georgia and the family moved to Marietta, Ga in March of 1941.

Initially the family moved into a large house on Forest Avenue with an apartment on the second floor. Housing was sparse because of the War and influx of Bomber Plant people. I remember this house as being big with a large yard for me to play in. It had a fish pond that was identified as a death threat to me if I fell in. I thoroughly enjoyed the yard and have not one memory of the interior of the apartment. After a short time we moved to Vance Circle.

During the War period President Roosevelt renewed measures to assure that prices were not escalated. The Office of Price Controls was one of these. This document represents how it applied to our rental of 123 Vance Circle from Mrs. Vance.

The **Office of Price Administration (OPA)** was established within the Office for Emergency Management of the United States Government by Executive Order 8875 on August 28, 1941. The functions of the OPA were originally to control prices (price controls) and rents after the outbreak of World War II.

Marietta 1939-1946

Fig. 68 Jack Sr., Gertrude, and Jackie ca. 1943

The time in Marietta was comfortable, exciting, and expansive as Jim was born there in 1943. This was War time in America. Fears, rationing, and changes in occupations were ever present. People were on the move as men and women entered the services and took jobs in the defense industry. Marietta was the home of the Bell Bomber Plant. It brought many new faces to the small town as well as the threat of attack from German destruction.

Fig. 69 Bell Bomber Plant

While the likelihood of flights from Germany to Georgia was low, it had to be a consideration. Everyone, including our family, observed curfew during air raid blackouts.

**Fig. 70 A B-29 flies over the Marietta Bell Bomber plant.
Kennesaw Mountain is visible in the background.**

We had black-out curtains on every window. When a raid was announced Mother and I would sit in a blacked out bathroom in the center of the house with all the lights out until the all-clear siren sounded. Dad was an Air Raid Warden and he donned his white helmet and went out to see where the flour bombs landed as well as seeing that that no one violated the curfew. Dad, Jack, volunteered for the draft on several occasions but was rejected as 4-F because of pulmonary symptoms. This rejection was a disappointment to him as he wanted to be a part of the War effort and not considered a special circumstance person. Mother was glad he did not have to leave for the service but supported him for his feelings. Dad took First Aid courses at the Red Cross and Warden training to "do his part" in the War effort.

For me the War described my play habits. I had a GI Joe doll with the U.S. Army uniform. I had soldiers and army cars and trucks to command. The grocery stores had balsa planes in the cereal boxes and paper planes as part of the back of the box. This made grocery shopping with Mother much more of an adventure.

Our home at 123 Vance Circle was a rented house with three bedrooms, living room, dining room and one central bath. The bathroom was a place for discipline if Jackie needed any. He was to sit alone there until he realized the error of his ways. This replaced any "switching" which was usually only a warning-"you go and get me a switch I am going to use on you". Very little of that behavior for me, an ideal child!

Fig. 71 123 Vance Circle, Marietta, GA. 1943

My Dad worked as a designer for McNeil Marble and Granite Company. Because of the war and rationing, he often would ride to work on a bicycle. We went to company picnics and on one occasion I recited the Pledge of Allegiance for the group. They dressed me up for these occasions. I sensed Dad was important and well liked at McNeil.

Fig. 72 McNeil Outing

My Dad was called Daddy or Little Daddy when Big Daddy was around. I never quite understood why Little Daddy was bigger than Big Daddy. Daddy took me to Saturday movies on the square. We bought Mommy's birthday present together and I picked out a glass candy jar which we still have. He took me to the high school football field where the Lone Ranger and Tonto were featured riding on their horses, Silver and Scout. Every evening he sat in his chair and me on the floorwhile we listened to radio and the Lone Ranger was never missed. It seemed he was as big a fan as I was.

Fig. 73 Hi Ho Silver, Git'um up Scout

Daddy carved wooden airplanes for me to play with too. One time I had a glass airplane which had been filled with candy and I was playing with it on the patio at the rear of the house. The family was sitting there enjoying the evening air. Jimmy was disturbed that he did not have an airplane and grabbed mine and threw it to the ground. Of course it broke into many pieces. I was greatly upset at this incident. Daddy immediately carved me a wooden one and put a propeller in front with a pin. The propeller twirled when I blew it. He usually used mother's fingernail polish to paint his projects. That solved my concern.

Our back yard was separated from a dirt road by a hedge and fence. Negros lived across the dirt road. One Negro boy about my age would come to the fence and we would visit from time to time. My best friend was Dale Wayne Covington who lived two houses down Vance Circle. Dale Wayne's Dad opened a store on that back road and we visited it to get Cokes and candy bars. His Dad had retired from teaching at the High School. One of his subjects for the High School Boys was Shop. In Shop they studied silhouettes of air planes so they could identify enemy planes if necessary. Mr. Covington had models of these silhouettes on his back porch and they were very intriguing to me.

Dale Wayne had a typewriter that we were allowed to use on rainy days. He also had carbon paper which was remarkable and we drew and typed many a copy at his house. I took my family to see Dale a few years ago and he still lived in the family house. He had attended GA Tech and taught there until retirement. He had one of the original Apple Computers he still used. My son John was impressed that Dale still used a crystal radio set he had made with homemade liquid batteries in place. He apparently became a brilliant but eccentric adult. We were great friends as children and I still hold warm memories of our times together. I believe he played High School Basketball and was very active in the First Baptist Church of Marietta. He and I attended Sunday School and Vacation Bible School there for several years. Dale Wayne and I were engaged in many pursuits. One popular activity in the spring was to catch honey bees in jars off Obelia bushes blooming in his yard. We hoped for a queen bee which we had never seen before.

Fig. 74 Jackie and Dale Wayne 1943

We shot arrows from small bows at targets in his yard. We explored the neighborhood and a small creek at the junction of North Forest Avenue and Vance Circle. This neighborhood was utopia for a boy of 7-9 years.

One person across from our house had a tennis court and swimming pool. We did not know them and never visited these intriguing sites. Leo Aikman, a journalist for the Atlanta Constitution lived down from Dale Wayne and Mother always told friends that fact.

[Leo Aikman, 1908-1978, was a columnist for the Atlanta Constitution from 1947 until his death. He also was a humorist and speaker who entertained and inspired audiences across the continental United States. Born in Dana, Ind., Dec. 22, 1908, he received his bachelor's degree at DePauw University and his master's degree in American History at the University of Michigan. He worked with the National Parks Service in Washington, D.C., for several years before transferring to Marietta, Ga., in 1941 as historian at Kennesaw Mountain National Battlefield Park. He began his newspaper career as editor of the weekly Cobb County Times in Marietta before joining the Atlanta Constitution in 1948.]

Elmo Smith lived two doors from Dale Wayne. He was older than us and an infrequent partner. I remember when I was learning to ride a two wheel bike; he offered to help me ride down his driveway. It seemed very steep at the time but has become flat with the passage of time. He said he would run along behind and keep me from tipping over. We did well until I looked back and saw that Elmo was standing in the driveway and I was in the street –another skinned knee.

Dad bought me an Irish Mail to ride. He said that he had one as a boy and it was a preferable ride to a tricycle. The Irish Mail had a seat with four wheels. The seat was steel. The front wheels were steered by the feet on each side. The locomotion was by a large bar for the hands to push and pull to activate a lever to the rear wheels. Dad said he could go up small hills with his Mail. I never could. The problem I understood then and now is that the power lever did not allow for any free-wheeling. Therefore there was no coasting, only powered movement. If one tried to coast downhill, the pull bar would thrash back and forth and hit the unwary rider in the chin. I struggled with the thing for months but never liked it the way Dad felt I should.

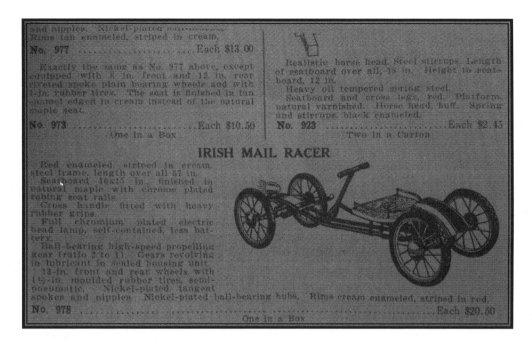

My Irish Mail did not have a headlight but it did have a formed metal seat. When Dad bought a new drill, he tried it out on the seat with a metal bit. It worked fine on the metal.

Before Jim was born I was an only child. That was great! Each morning Mom and I marched around the dining room table to the music of Don McNeil's Breakfast Club. Mom, the Kindergarten graduate, gave me flags to carry on the march.

The 1942 Breakfast Club Family Album

> **Curator's note**: The Family Albums Don McNeill produced for a number of years were one of the factors in the success of the "Breakfast Club". They facilitated the bonding between the show and its audience. And they reinforced the element of "family" that the show projected. The 1942 yearbook, distributed during some of the darkest days of World War II, is especially interesting to read in these times of a much different war (or perhaps wars).

I had a Cocker Spaniel named Ginger and colored the same. I loved her as my first pet. I had two other friends in Marietta and hold them in fond memories today. They were Guck and Tappy, imaginary boys. Guck was a serious friend and gave me advice and caution when needed. Tappy was a joyful, laughing person. He was adventurous and uplifting. We never knew where they came from or where they went when Jimmy was born. I guess they went to play with some other "only boy child" who did not have a brother.

Another friend lived in a brown cedar shingled house up the street on North Forest Avenue. His dad was an FBI agent I was told. (This was to a second grade student) One day we were swinging on his backyard swing set and the chain broke while I was swinging. I remember this as the first sense of horror and fear I ever knew. My pal told me I had broken his swing and his Dad, the FBI man, was going to get me. I ran home and into my room in the back of the house. I pulled the chest of drawers in front of the door and hid under the bed. I do not remember how I recovered but I did not have to go to the penitentiary. Incidentally, my aunt Billy Butterworth Campbell, was an artist like my Dad. She visited us one time in Marietta and painted Indian designs on my chest of drawers and painted the rest white. I enjoyed that chest for years after. I had much attention from aunts and grandmothers.

While in Marietta I became sick with Scarlet Fever. This was a feared childhood disease at the time because antibiotics were only beginning to become available. Our home was quarantined with a red sign on the front door. Dad could go to work but he and Mom could not enter my room. I was put in the front bedroom. They put towels and basins of antiseptic on the threshold of the door and I was confined to one room. I used a bedpan and stayed in bed. They put Clorox in the bed pans to suppress the bacteria in the urine and stool. My grandmother Burr, Viola Newby, came to town announcing that she did not care about the quarantine and she was staying with me in the room. She moved in and cared for me for the weeks I was imprisoned. I don't remember any fever or pain. I do remember the volume of toys and especially soldiers I received as sick gifts. Scarlet Fever is an infection of Streptococcus which can affect the kidneys and heart. So far as I know I did not get any sequelae and am now 73 years old. Time enough to show up I would think. I was given the new drug, Sulfathiazole. I guess it shocked the Streptococcus which had not had time to become resistant in 1942.

My parent's friends were named Kingsley and Doris Miller. We visited their house many times and the adults played bridge. The Millers had two sons. Later I re-met one of them at the UGA Chi Phi House where he was known as Red-Eye Miller. We played in the hedges behind his house on Kennesaw Avenue near the railroad tracks- very good memories. Their neighborhood was one of my favorite in Marietta. There were large yards, sidewalks, and large homes. The street lights were particularly attractive round globes on green metal poles-a very neighborly hood. Mr. Miller ran a frozen food house or packing house. We visited there on Sunday rides occasionally.

The Marietta town square was wonderful. Dad and I walked there to go to the western movie shows on many a Saturday. The square attracted large droves of blackbirds and the benches were always dotted with bird poop. On the corner was a drug store with a wonderful marble fountain bar. We got drinks there or ice cream cones. One of my early traumatic experiences occurred in that drug store. Mom parked in front of the store and let me go in alone to get ice cream cones for us. I was given a 50 cent piece which I knew was a large amount of money. After ordering, I stood at the counter, quite high for me then, and tapped the coin on the marble counter. It jumped loose and fell down a crack in the marble. There was no recovery. I began crying at my mistake and loss. A man sitting at a table gave me a quarter but that was not enough to replace my great loss. Another early scar in life's journey!

Another adventure was the time my Mother let me off on the square to go to the dentist alone. She was to go on another errand and meet me in the dentist office on the second floor. You can see how safe life was in those days as my mother was a good and careful person. I was to get an examination only to see if a molar needed to be pulled. Mother told me I would not get an extraction since this dentist had had a fatality with an extraction earlier and would not do any more. However when she arrived at the office, I had undergone an extraction and was in good shape. I reminded her of that story years later. I was about 9 at the time.

Fig. 75 Jackie, Gertrude, Jimmy

Front porch 123 Vance Circle, Marietta GA. Ca. 1944

Fig. 76 Schooldays

Our school was within walking distance and we carried our empty bookbags daily.

I recall the smell of wooden pencils in the sharpener and of the erasers. We had Blue Horse writing pads and made new friends. I especially remember a girl named Shirley Landers who was a friend. I always wondered how her life turned out. I stayed at that school until midway through the second grade when we moved to Athens, GA.

Fig. 77 Jackie's First Grade

One of the events in Marietta was the parade on Confederate Memorial Day. Our school lined up on the square and marched with small flags to the Confederate Cemetery. There were many people in the parade and it seemed a long march. We placed the flags on the markers of the men buried there.

Fig. 78 Confederate Cemetery, Marietta, Georgia Begun 1863

The Confederate Cemetery is located off Powder Spring Street in Marietta, Georgia. There are 3,000 Confederate dead from every southern state buried in this cemetery. Many of these are unknown and relatively few have information on their markers. First established for Confederate soldiers killed in a railroad collision in September 1863, it became the resting place for dead from nearby battlefields. In 1866, under the direction of Miss Mary J. Green and Mrs. Charles J. Williams of the Georgia Memorial Association, bodies were moved here from the Chickamauga and Ringgold battlefields.

James Newby Butterworth was born in Marietta. I remember walking with Dad to the hospital and remarking how Jimmy had no neck. He was very young while we lived there and has few memories of that time. He was too young to be involved with me and Dale Wayne but always present at home. We played as best one could with a 1-2 year old but I guess I was too young for much responsibility.

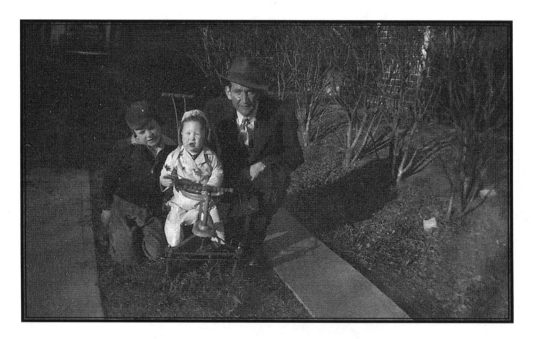

Fig. 79 Butterworth Boys 1943

One sad day I was told we would have to move from Vance Circle. We had offered our front room to a young woman border. She had a boyfriend who picked her up on a motorcycle which was quite exciting to me. One day I was told the boy was killed on his motorcycle. After she moved, the lady who owned the house came back to town and wanted to move into her house. She moved into the border's room for a few weeks as we searched for another home. I was devastated that we were leaving our home and I would have to leave Dale Wayne and Vance Circle. Dad and Mother found a house close by on Forest Avenue. The house had burned previously and had been restored. It still smelled like fire. Behind the back yard was a lot where a young girl kept her horse. I liked the horse and the odor of the horse lot. I remember the girl as being pretty with dark hair. The life in that house was never as happy as at 123 Vance Circle.

One more friend the family had was the Johnson family. They lived some distance from either house and we visited often. They may have lived in a complex for military workers. We have several pictures of Peggy Johnson as we were good friends and she was a very cute little girl-just my age.

Fig. 80   Jackie and Peggy Johnson 1943

Her Dad was named Math Johnson but I forget her mother's name. The mother died with breast cancer I believe. They visited us much later in Gainesville on one occasion when we lived on North Bradford Street.

Fig. 81   Jimmy, Peggy Johnson, and Jackie 301 North Bradford Street, Gainesville, Ga

I want to mention a few words about the automobile we had in Marietta. It was a 1938 Chevrolet Sedan. It was much like the one on the left of this picture.

Fig. 82 1938 Chevy

I never heard where or how Dad got the car but it was not new to us. It had "mohair" seat covers and the cotton would wedge out at the corners of the seats especially if a small boy picked at it. The trunk was upright rather than flat. The heater was very inefficient so we always carried blankets on our trips to Atlanta or Vienna. Remember this was wartime so we had to have coupons for gas and tires. The tires were not good and may have been made out of some synthetic material.

> *{In 1940, Franklin Roosevelt, calling rubber a "strategic and critical material," creates the Rubber Reserve Company (RRC), to stockpile natural rubber and regulate synthetic rubber production. Firestone, B.P. Goodrich, Goodyear, and U.S. Rubber agree to work together to solve the nation's wartime rubber needs.}*

Tires had inner tubes and Dad was skilled in applying patches to the tubes when punctured. Several methods were available, a cold patch and a hot patch. I remember watching Dad light a match to the edge of the patch to enhance the bonding.

> *{"Everyone carried a tube and tire repair kit, plus a jack and an air pump. The early tube repair kits were for "hot" patches, but the later ones were for "cold" patches. Dad always carried a pair of tin snips to cut whatever size patch he needed. The patch material came in a special metal can and it's lid looked like a grater on top, because the inner tube had to be "roughed up" in order for the patch to stick securely to the glue, which was applied over the rough spot."}*

Jennie, Gas Rationing in WWII, Internet Quote

On the highway it was not uncommon to see or to be involved in stopping and repairing tires. Our car was a practical conveyance and not a status symbol of any degree. It was used for necessary trips and occasional Sunday rides if we had the stamps for gas. I do not remember ever a discussion about whether this was a good or bad car, just our car. Mother drove it as well as Dad and she was the one who drove us to Athens when we moved.

Dad sold the Chevy Sedan after we had been in Athens for a while since he had a Chevrolet Coupe from his work and we did not need two cars. After he sold it he said we did not want to see it again as the purchaser had refurbished it, painted it tan, and it looked very snazzy. He did not want us to be regretful it was sold I guess.

Another conveyance of note was the electric Street Car in Atlanta. There were also some in Marietta. The tracks remained for some years after the Cars were gone. Electric buses took its place. I remember traveling from Atlanta to Marietta on a Street Car. I cannot believe it was electric all that way but I don't know another energy source.

{*"Less than twenty miles from downtown Atlanta, Marietta was connected by streetcar, by the Dixie Highway, and by the state's first four-lane highway, U.S. 41, then under construction."*} Advertisement for Marietta, Georgia

Before the turn of the century Atlanta had a Street-railway using horses and mules to pull the cars. The streets were mostly dirt at that time. I remember Big Daddy riding with me and us seeing the roadside shops selling novelties and drinks as we passed going to Marietta. I thought we were a-way out in the mountains.

Athens, Georgia 1946-1948

We moved from Forest Avenue in Marietta to Athens, Ga midway of my Second Grade school year. My Mother made the move seem like an adventure. I did not want to leave Marietta, my friends, school, church, and childhood utopia. But here came this adventure of meeting new friends, starting at a new school, and living in a new house. She made it seem exciting and that was good because we <u>were</u> going to move. We found a great house at 295 Hodgson Drive and I quickly forgot any regret for Marietta. Over the following years I have speculated what it would have been like to grow up in Marietta or Athens either for that matter. It would have been good with different opportunities than those I met in Gainesville. In Marietta I was sheltered by community and age. In Athens I became more exposed to competition, interaction with older boys, sports, and music.

Our road, Hodgson Drive, was not paved at that time. They coated it with oil from time to time to keep the dust down. That seemed appropriate and just fine to me. Our house had two bedrooms, one for parents and one for Jackie and Jimmie. One bathroom stood between them. Off the living room we had a small room with windows all around that served for a single guest on occasion. If we had a couple to visit, Mother and Dad would put a pallet in the living room for me and Jimmy or they themselves would sleep there and give their room to the guests-usually relatives. I understood the giving up of your bed to guests as the way it was to be done most of my life.

Cousin Newby Kelt transferred from VMI to UGA after we left Marietta. He moved into the small porch room with the windows. It was great for him to be with us and we pitched footballs and baseballs with him and Dad.

Fig. 83 Jimmy and Newby ca. 1946

Newby later moved to other quarters. He was studying Forestry. He was on the UGA wrestling team and the football team for a while. He dated Coach Wally Butt's daughter, Nancy, for a time and Wally recruited him so I remember.Newby became a Naval Aviator, wining the Flying Cross years later, and retired from the Navy as a Commander.

Fig. 84 Coach Wally Butts

Coach and athletic director at the University of Georgia for more than two decades, **Wally Butts** helped to shape the football careers of Hall of Famers Frank Sinkwich, Charley Trippi, and Fran Tarkington. Perhaps more importantly, Butts instilled a sense of values and discipline in all the young men who passed through his football program at Georgia.

Kenneth Carter lived across the street and was a year ahead of me in school. We were best friends for our whole time in Athens and I respected him as an older boy. We played with Buddy Chapman and his brother who lived next to Kenneth. Kenneth had a great "funny book" collection and enjoyed toy cars with me.

Between the roots of large trees are the best sites for making parking sites for toy cars. There was sandy soil between the roots allowing good scraping and smoothing of the surface. Kenneth and I liked his front yard which had such a tree-probably an Oak. A collection of colored cars of varying designs was the pinnacle of ownership! They were not replicas of any cars of the times, 1946-1948. But they had their own style. One of my most memorable was a red two-seater that had swept back front fenders. Most of our collection was made out of metal, probably lead cast. But some were rubber cars and were larger than our favorite ones. Occasionally we got trucks. Some were miniature car carrying trucks with tiny cars on board. Those were not especially good for rolling and parking on the sandy dirt roads.

Buddy Chapman and his little brother lived next to Kenneth. They played with us sometimes. They had a great creek in their back yard. One time I got interested in boats and had a great wooden cruiser that I floated in the creek. Crawdads were in that creek and we watched them and caught them with our hands. They were too small for the pinchers to cause any pain. We made dams for the boats to float in and sometimes go over the break in the dam. That same creek ran behind the Speering's house. I went to their house and played with Geraldine, who was older, and her brother Robin. One time we were in a tree over the creek climbing into the branches. I was a fair climber but not so good at getting down. On this occasion I reached up to a branch and saw a green snake right at my hand. I panicked and jumped all the way down to a large rock in the middle of the creek. I did not stop running until I got to my house. That event remains in my memory as a frightful experience, my third.

The street running parallel to Hodgson Drive off King Avenue was Matthews Avenue where we went to play football sometimes. I remember a boy named Parson and Jack Prather who played with us. They were older than me. There were fields of "broom straw" on that street that was plentiful in the fall. I liked the way it waved in the breezes from time to time and that memory still gives me pleasurable sensations.

All the boys I knew belonged to the Athens YMCA. It was the most impressive organization for boys I ever knew. It still is today.

Fig. 85 Athens "Y"

I remember Coburn Frasier Kelly as the leader of the "Y" when we were there in 1946-1948. I encourage anyone interested to read the Y history at the link: http://www.athensymca.org/history.shtml

Coach Kelly had us third graders march into his office and he pronounced our football position. He said "you are a Right Tackle". And that was it for me. I joined the favored team of Billy Slaughter who was a year older than me and going to another school. The other team was led by Tommy Carteau. I was told Carteau was noted for the "line buck". My job was to stop him. We scrimmaged on the field behind the Y several days a week. I loved that game during my second, third and fourth grade years. One year we played Fritz Orr School or Camp, a group from Atlanta. The game was just before kickoff of a UGA game at Sanford Stadium. Now that was a big deal! I got to play some in the game and we won. On one occasion there was an award party at the Y. We actually took girls to it. I took Susan Parsons who was in my school class and lived up the street from us on Sunset Drive. Some of the better players were given a silver football on a small chain. They gave them to their girl friends. How I would have liked to have gotten one of those.

One interesting story told to me after I left Athens concerned another Atlanta Team coming to Athens for a game. Apparently there was some mix-up in the scheduling and the Team from Atlanta arrived in their bus at the Y on a Saturday prepared to play football. No "Y" team was present and no one knew a game was scheduled. The Atlanta team had flashy uniforms and was very well prepared. With their arrival, some boys went into the Y building and began recruiting others to play the Atlanta boys. They did not have matching jerseys but they all did have some equipment at the "Y". With this ragged team, the game began. I am sure the Atlanta team thought they were very mismatched. And indeed they were.They returned to Atlanta with their fancy uniforms and a Loss in their column to an Athens YMCA "pick-up" team.

When Gainesville High played Athens in 1954, several boys I knew at the "Y" were on the Athens Team. They had played together since 2nd grade. I remembered names of Slaughter, Simpson,

Rowland, Towns, and others I have since forgotten. Later when UGA won the SEC championship in 1960, some of those names were on the Georgia roster.

I went to school at Chase Street School located on Chase Street of course. It was a bit down the hill off Prince Avenue, a large street in Athens. This was a great time in my memory. Jimmy had not started school when we lived in Athens. Mrs. Rowland was the principal and Mrs. Means was my third grade teacher, Mrs. Tabor my fourth grade teacher. My mother thought that I should skip the Third Grade and we talked to Mrs. Means about that. She felt that I would do better to stay in my class. I was a few months older than my class since my birthday was at the end of December and most classmates had birthdays in June to September. But if I went ahead, I would have been that much younger than the majority. So I stayed where I was. At Sunday School they put me in the older class so I always went to Sunday School with boys in the class ahead of me.

Chase Street School and the Boys Choir were special to me. There were several activities at that school. One I remember was when Dad made me a kite to enter in a contest Kites at the school one March. He drew an eagle on the paper and it was the greatest kite in the show. The Speerings had tiny kites and won the smallest kite contest. I think we won something but don't remember what prize. We should have gotten first prize because it was a beautiful one and flew well. Dad taught me how to use sticks we gathered in fields around the neighborhood to make kites. The best choices were ones that had a hollow center and were light. We usually made a plain T shaped kite with a string bowing the cross piece to keep it from dipping. We tore rags and tied them together for the tail. He was particular about the size and length of the tail. Uncle Fred Turner brought us a big bolt of twine they used in the hosiery mill and we could almost send a kite out of sight. We sent messages up the string but I don't know who got them. Dad said that Box Kites were the best and would fly without dipping down. We never made one of those that I remember-just wished we had one to try.

Chase Street School was built in a square with a central court yard. We went to first recess in the middle court yard for a short recess and in the back yard for the second recess after lunch. I don't remember a lunch room so maybe we took our lunches.

The Chase Street Boys Choir was famous in town and we made a record of our songs. I remember names like "Madame Jeannette" and "In My Dear Green Cathedral". We walked to the church on Prince Avenue one Thanksgiving for our concert. We were Great! Laddie Wiggley I recall was a good singer and had special parts. I was good but not that good.

Fig. 86 Chase Street Boy's Choir 1947

From time to time Mother would take us to the McClellan's, Mc Crory's or Kress's store we knew as "Ten Cent" stores. That was the haven of toy cars. Those stores had a very special smell to them. The one in Vienna had that smell and was a treasure site for many purchases. In Vienna I was given money because it kept me from bothering adults and they wanted me to enjoy my visits. So I was off to the 10cents store. In Athens I could go to town on the bus which stopped at the end of Hodgson Drive. I remember taking it on one occasion with a friend who was a girl. No romance involved, just a friend. She had a pony in her back yard and that made her special. She was a rugged sort for a girl and wore special riding pants sometimes. This time we went to town I saw a Negro girl I knew at the back of the bus. She was the daughter of Annie B. Hester who stayed with my brother and me. I went back and talked with her on the ride to town leaving my friend in our seats. Later I was told that was not good behavior.

Athens had a great magazine store in the middle of town. It was open to the sidewalk and had a long display of magazines. This store had its special odor also, like news print I later learned. There were racks of "funny books" there and almost always I could get two or three to take home. I collected them and Kenneth and I swapped books. Whoever had the largest stack was special. Big Little Books were popular too. They were hard backed, half the size of "funny books', and had small pictures in the upper right hand corner so that when you flipped the pages, they became a "movie". My brother Jimmy and Freddy may have had collections but they were too young to understand Marvel Comics and the like.

Dad worked at the Athens Marble and Granite Company on the Atlanta Road, not too far from our house. I think he was offered a partnership position with time but that did not work out. This was a better opportunity than staying at McNeil's in Marietta I was told. He liked the people he worked for and on occasion we went on picnics with Mr. Brazille and his family. They had a daughter close to my age who was pretty.One of Mother and Dad's friends was a druggist and we visited with them often. They lived on Prince Avenue past the Normal School where Mother had attended college. They had two daughters close to my and Jimmy's age. We enjoyed those visits.

Our next door neighbor was Fred Bell who owned Bell's Grocery Store. Their son Freddie was Jimmy's age and they were good friends. They had a Negro yard- man who cut their grass with a motorized lawn mower, the first in my memory. It was new of him too and on one occasion it ran off from him causing quite a stir in the neighborhood.

Jimmy and I enjoyed that neighborhood. We could play cowboys on the rocks in a vacant lot behind our house, play cards with the girls next door, and generally enjoy home life. Often our parents would sit in the back yard in the evening and enjoy the twilight gleaming. That was pleasant. Annie B. Hester was Mother's help one day a week. She liked to listen to soap operas on the radio and we listened too. Pepper Young's Family was one I remember along with Lum and Abner.

Fig.87 Annie B. Hester

When I had the Chickenpox I developed a significant itching during the night. In the dark I went to the bathroom and called to Mother that I was going to put Calamine Lotion on my itching. She was in bed and said to go ahead. The next morning they discovered I had painted myself with white shoe polish instead. It seemed to help the itching anyway. I was quite the story for a few years after that escapade.

At the end of my fourth grade year, my aunt Sity invited me to spend the summer with her in New York. She lived in Bayside, Queens, Long Island. I got permission from Mrs. Rowland and Mrs. Tabor to leave a week before school was out and we went to New York on the Silver Comet. It was a famous train in 1948 and passed through Athens, GA. I think it was a Southern Railroad train. Aunt Sity (Audrey) and I had a Pullman Sleeping car and ate meals in the dining car. It was a wonderful trip. I stayed several weeks and we went to New York City on the subway and the elevated trains. My cousin Mary Kelt Kiser lived close to her parents and we went to her apartment often. She had a television and I had not seen one before. Patrick Mc Garity was an older boy than me but he took me sailing and we saw baseball games on his TV at his house. Aunt Sity was the perfect hostess. We went to the Bronx Zoo, Radio City Music Hall, and several radio shows before dining in a Chinese Restaurant. Uncle Jack helped me with model airplanes and I helped him with his garden and putting up storm windows, which we did not have in Athens or Marietta GA. Uncle Jack had a perfectly planned shop and he had me keep my part clean too. On the way back to GA, Sity and I stopped by Mt. Vernon and Washington, DC for the tours. She wanted to be sure her nephews had a firsthand education at a young age. This was a valuable experience and well thought out by Sity and Mom. In later years my brother Jim and Cousin Johnny Pharr took the same trip with her.

On return from NYC on the Silver Comet, which I made alone with a tag on my shirt from Washington DC, we moved to Gainesville GA and began a new course of life. It was not good to leave Athens and friends. But, again, Mom made it seem like an adventure and it became an exciting time for all of us.

Gainesville Ga 1948-2007

Dad accepted an offer from Alfred Fletcher of Gainesville Marble and Granite Company in Gainesville GA to become a Manager and Designer. Alfred's wife Mary Fannie was a Butterworth. It is my understanding that Dad expected again to become a partner in the business after a period of time. One of Alfred's sons, Jack Fletcher, worked there also. It was my opinion that the business flourished after Dad arrived because he added a sense of sophistication to the operation and was able to design the Monuments "in house". We often visited with the Fletchers and watched many bouts of Professional Wrestling on their TV. They had two sons, Junior, who was wheel chair confined, and Eugene who was in my class at High School. I worked in Junior's store one week in the summer. It was a community store constructed of concrete blocks. He sold tobacco products, soft drinks, crackers etc. I didn't mind the work and Junior was friendly and helpful. He was about 6 years older than I was at the time. Another Butterworth lived in the Fletcher's house at the time but I don't remember the name. I do know my Big Mama did not care for that family. I don't know the history of that story. The Fletchers had a Parrott in a cage and it contributed to the conversation from time to time. Herb Butterworth, a recently identified cousin, told this story about the Parrot. One day a man appeared at the house door announcing that he had a load of firewood and where was he to put it. A voice called out, "just put it in the back". He unloaded the wood and left. Later Alfred came home and wanted to know where the wood had come from. They later figured that the Parrot, the only one in the house at the time in question, had directed the man where to place the delivery.

After a few years there was a parting of the ways with the Fletchers. It seemed that Alfred felt Dad was taking too much control of the operation. He was offered a position with Carroll Daniel Construction Company and a subsidiary company named Gainesville Sheet Metal Company. Later he moved to the primary Construction Company site and that was the best move of this career in my opinion.

He became a home and business designer and engineer. That prepared him to later open his own business and privately do design work from home. At Carroll Daniel he was popular with Carroll and they worked together well.

Dad was never interested in Civic Clubs but he visited at Kiwanis and Rotary from time to time. They did not appeal to him. He was involved with the Youth Center at the Civic Building and designed their Center. His friends in Gainesville were Byron Davis, John Gibbons, Wade Lindorme, and Colquitt Perry among others. They met from time to time, walked at the Mall, and visited as couples. I think most of these friendships resulted as wife-contacts. They all joined in for Bridge parties with the wives and talking politics.

We initially moved into a large old house at 301 North Bradford Street. It had been made into a duplex by Mr. Plexico who owned it and rented it out. Mom said houses were difficult to find because of the post War rush. Many people had to find temporary housing at that time I was told.

Fig. 88 301 North Bradford 1949

The Gibbons family lived in the smaller duplex. Their daughters Lynn and Cheryl were present but rarely part of our play group. John and Evelyn Gibbons were two of my parent's best friends in life.

We had lots of room outside and inside. But he heat was not good. I recall Dad and me going under the house in winter to put up insulation. It was 4 degrees outside. We used coal and wood burning stoves in the dining room and the central foyer. I sometimes split oak wood logs dad bought. They did not split well because the wood had no cleavage plane and this was not a happy chore.

A vacant lot next door was overgrown with Kudzu. Behind that was the "red hole". That Wonder was a steep bank leading to a large lot without vegetation. After Friday afternoon Cowboy movies, we replayed the adventures in the Red Hole and came home coated with Georgia red dust. There were some roots remaining on the bank of the Red Hole and this allowed us to pull up from the deep bottom and climb up to the level of the lot next door to our house. That climb always resulted in a real severe coating of red clay.

The front yard was a small one but large enough to require grass cutting with the iron wheeled reel push lawn mower we got from Big Mama. It had a small bank that allowed us to attempt 'flying" after Friday Superman movies by pinning towels around our necks. We gained altitude only in our minds. Roger, who lived with his grandmother across Bradford, played and went to the movies with us nearly every weekend. We continued to play with cars in the back yard and the sandy soil and Oak tree roots still served us well. At this point in life cars were becoming less interesting.

I acquired a pair of white rabbits for Easter one year and that led to Dad making me a rabbit hutch in the back yard. We harvested many rabbits from that hobby. We never sold any except babies for Easter presents occasionally. We never ate any of those rabbits, only ones we shot on hunts. I gave several away. One large Buck escaped into the Kudzu field next door while I let him feed on outside diet. The hutch required cleaning often and that was my job of course. Maggots would grow in the under- layer of feces if I went too long without cleaning. The pen was not designed for cleaning and it was strictly manual labor of the undesirable kind. Jim was around but I don't recall getting much help with this job from him-he may disagree. Harold Hogsed visited and liked the rabbit business. He started his own hutch with brown rabbits. I don't know how long he raised his but mine went on for a few years.

Our house had a two tiered stairway to the second floor. Upstairs we had three rooms. Mom and Dad were in one, Jim and me in another, and one vacant. One year we rented to a young couple but I don't remember their names. I do remember them wrestling on the bed on occasion and that looked like a fun experience to me. I guess they were recently married.

Jim and I played in an upstairs porch area that had small window panes fronting onto Bradford Street. A few of those were broken but we never replaced them. It was mostly for storage. Our bedroom was large with one large closet. No bathrooms were on the second floor and we all used a single bath off the kitchen. I do remember the lack of heat in the winter as no rooms had heat, only what arose from the central foyer downstairs.

We used a table in the foyer hall for meals when we did not use the dining room. It was also for projects and studying. The dining room had a bed for guests and a wood stove. It had a small porch off the north side which was good for air rifle practice.

The basement was a great place. It was large and had a dirt floor. One section was probably meant for growing plants as it had a sidewall of windows. I used it for a chemistry lab. I thoroughly enjoyed that room. As we age we regret that today's youth does not get to enjoy our experiences. But remember, they have their own which are just as meaningful in their own life-view. We are all so fortunate to be able to relive the lies of youth.

The garage was large enough for two or three cars. It had a hardwood floor for some reason and was a great place to skate and ride a bike. We had several bikes, mostly second hand. I traveled everywhere on them. We put playing cards on the fender straps and the spokes made a sound like a motorcycle. I rode to Candler Street School either going up Green Street, the easy way, or up Bradford which had a large hill. On practice days I balanced my trombone case on the handle bars with no problem. We rode out to Riverside or to New Holland when the need arose and all over our town.

Fig. 89 Bradford Street Workshop

One year we became entrepreneurial by bringing pecans back from Vienna and shelling them for the candy company down the street. Two brothers lived at the bottom of Bradford Street and operated a candy store. We packaged our nuts in cellophane bags and sold them there. It gave us pocket change but took a long time even with all the family shelling. We had another family venture when Dad invented a cover for cigarettes which held a pack of paper matches. The idea was to put a pack in the folder and you had matches always conveniently available. These had the logo of the company giving them out and were to be a great advertisement tool. They were printed in sheets of cardboard and required folding to give to the advertiser. Our family folded many of these at the table in the foyer. Later Marlboro came out with the cardboard pack and the venture lost prominence. We hoped Dad would reach fortune and fame with this great idea, but it was too late in the evolution of cigarette marketing.

Other than those two ventures, we sold subscriptions for magazines, greeting cards, and later encyclopedias with little success by me. Jim did well with a newspaper route. Jim would get up with

Mother early in the morning and fold newspapers and deliver them. This went on for a few years it seemed with many early morning rides. I worked as a teenager at the Big Star sacking groceries. I made 50 cents an hour on Friday and Saturdays. There also were tips for carrying the bags to the cars. Mr. Flannagan was the manager and also the father of June Flannagan who was in our dating group. I was very embarrassed one Saturday when I showed up for work in a white tee shirt and jeans. He sent me home to get a real shirt as the tee was not acceptable at the Big Star. We only lived a half block from the Big Star so it was not difficult to make the change. I had just made an embarrassing mistake in dressing for the public. That requirement has changed dramatically since the 1950s.

Jim and I rode bicycles down to the Big Star when it was closed and circled the parking lot. It was a lazy ride and we thought it was great. Sometimes we took a side trip to Mr. Emmett's furniture store and circled his lot too. One could make lazy figure of eights in the large lots

When I entered the 8th Grade I went to Gainesville High. At that time we were Sub-Freshmen but still in High School. My family moved to 247 North Avenue, N.E. that summer. I was thrilled as we were next door to my good friend Carl Romberg. Carl and I had many great times together as the years developed. The first summer we ran a wire from his room to mine and installed a used intercom he got from his family's Ice Company so we could talk to each other. His father had a shop in the basement and we used the jig saw and lathe for projects. This helped me in Industrial Arts later as I already had lathe skills. Carl and I were very active in Scouts and were both in Troop 26 of the First Baptist Church. We went on many Camporees and Summer camps together and finally got our Eagle Rank together.

Fig. 90 Troop 26, First Baptist Church 1950

One summer Mother drove us to Mount Oglethorpe to begin a hike on the Appalachian Trail. There were about six of us Scouts with no leaders. Our mission was to hike the Trail in Georgia and to do maintenance. We ended up at Neel's Gap a week later where another leader took up the mission. I remember Slaughter Gap and Blood Mountain as the most difficult part of the Trail to climb in Georgia. We met a fellow traveler on the Trail by the name of Dick Lamb. He wore shorts ,tennis shoes, and carried a very small pack. This outfit was compared to our jeans, hiking boots, and 40 lb ski packs. He only ate oatmeal soaked in water. He was traveling the entire Trail to Maine. We had maps to follow and stopped to cut logs from across the Trail from time to time. Dick was a scavenger and ate our leftovers as we had canned goods and bread. When we crossed highways where picnic tables and trash cans were present, he robbed them with gusto. I threw away a jar of blackberry jelly one time and he grabbed it and wiped it out with his finger to get the last bit. Often Dick got lost and met us at camp in the evening. The next year at school we had to write an essay on a theme from Reader's Digest called "The Most Unforgettable Person I have ever met". I used Dick Lamb for my topic and got an "A" from Mrs. Pentecost.

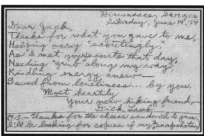

Andy Carter, Albert Hardy and Harold Hogsed were other friends that formed a close group to grow up together, Carl and I lived on North Avenue and Andy and Albert on Dixon Drive two blocks away. We carried our friendship into dating years. Carl and I double dated quite often. He married Betty Newnan, his regular date.

Billy Hood and his sister Betty Ann were older and lived on the other side of our house. Mr. Hood owned the house we rented. Billy became an Eagle before us. He also was on the football team playing End. We all played touch football and softball in the neighborhood in our yards or in the "deep hole" next to Carl's house. We had softball games in the lot next to the Coca Cola plant on Green Street in the spring. Harold Hogsed, Tommy Reins, and Howell Mendenhall were good friends and played with us often. They all lived in Longstreet Hills. I well remember each Easter getting a new glove, softball, or bat from the Easter Bunny. The smell of those items was wonderful. We had all gone to Candler Street School on Candler Street before High School. We held skating parties and bicycle parties when we were at Candler Street on Saturdays with our friends Nancy Wofford, Mary Ann Bedford, Margaret Cromartie, Diane Davis, Beth Bennett, Camille Brown and Thelma Clay. We later learned to dance together and enjoyed Church hayrides in the summer.

As I grew older I worked at Mr. Hood's furniture store, our neighbor on North Avenue. I moved furniture and accompanied the delivery person to deliver washing machines and stoves. Laying linoleum was a skilled procedure as it had to be formed around the appliances and lie flat. I was the helper on these jobs.

As a result of working at my Uncle Joe's drug store in Vienna, I got a job as soda jerk at the Imperial Drug Store. I knew how to make the shakes, sundaes, and fountain cokes. The disappointing aspect was that I somehow sensed an inferiority position to those High School students being served. I know now that is an unhealthy feeling and many kids today work at McDonalds and enjoy their relationships. I knew at school I was superior in grades to many being served so this was a change for me.

In later years I worked with the Highway Department and the Department of Agriculture as a Rodman and Bush Axe man clearing sight lines. All of these jobs required political contacts and my parents friends helped get these for me. None paid very well but it was summer work. The best job for summer in Gainesville was to work on a chicken truck. It paid $1.40 per hour which was very good. The truck left at 4 AM and returned about 3 PM giving the afternoon off. The workers went into the chicken houses and caught chickens and put them into wooden crates. They then loaded them onto the truck. Ronnie Hughes had such a job and lost much weight during that summer. It was not an easy job. I never got one of those jobs because I did not have a contact to get hired.

For my sophomore and Junior years I had to go to football practice much of the summer. We had morning and afternoon practice so my jobs were limited. After morning practice, we went downtown to the Collegiate Grill for a Big Orange drink. Walt Snelling, a popular and large Guard, had a Lincoln Zephyr Coupe. We piled into and onto the car with many of us riding on the fenders and on the running board. Off down Green Street we went. We were never questioned by any police. I walked home after the outing. I was thrilled to be included in the group which included many of the starting team, Walt Snelling, Gruesome Blackwell, and Wallace Russell. Doug Skelton, my friend, stayed near the Grill to play pool. Doug was a "pool shark" of some note and augmented his earnings in that practice.

Only one job I ever had was difficult and that was with the Hiwassee Land Company. I got that the summer I finished college. I needed money for a microscope to go to medical school. The job consisted of walking ahead of a D 7 Dozier and marking a compass line for the driver. I sprayed paint on the trees and he followed me with a sprayer on the tractor blasting herbicide and killing hardwoods. We met at the yard at 4 AM each morning. We loaded the tractor on the bed of a large truck and chained it down. Then we left for the site. I drove the big truck with 15 gears requiring double clutching to change gears. I had never driven anything like that before but got OJT that summer. We came back in the evening and unloaded and cleaned up the equipment preparing for the next morning. I got home about 10 PM each day and fell into the bath tub. That job paid well. Near the end of the summer I simply had to quit. I felt worn out and needed a few weeks off before school. My partner was a Russian emigrant and we became good friends that summer. I sold him a Compton encyclopedia and he was delighted to have it. I bought a $75 used single lens microscope for school and kept it for my entire course. I only got a binocular scope when I opened practice in Bristol 15 years later. Some of that summer's money went to buy a 1953 Chevrolet Bellaire hard top. This was in 1961. It had a rusted out rear quarter panel but otherwise in good shape. Cost was $225.00. I named it the Golden Rocket and it served me well for three years and I sold it to my brother Jimmy for $100.00.

Mother taught school for many years in Gainesville. She began at Miller Park on the southwest end of town. She taught the second grade. During her early years she had to attend summer school to upgrade her "certificate" since she did not have a four year degree. She and Peggy Olson became great friends and they taught together for years. Peggy was single as her husband had died in the war. She drove Mother to school much of the time. They both made friends with the Principal and children who remembered them for years.

Miller Park School Mrs. Butterworth's Second Grade 1954-55

Fig. 91 Mrs. Butterworth's Second Grade, Miller Park School 1954-1955

Later Mother decided to return to College and went to North Georgia College in Dahlonega. She commuted daily and finally graduated in her Cap and Gown. Around that time she transferred to Enota Elementary School which was closer to home on North Avenue. The Principal there was Leon Hughes who had moved from teaching History at the High School to become Principal. He was the brother of one of my best friends Ronnie Hughes. Mother continued teaching either a regular schedule or later as a substitute teacher in Elementary or even at the High School until she was in her 80's. She really enjoyed teaching. After retirement she continued to volunteer to teach reading to adults. She attended Brenau College Adult education up until the end of her life. She never lost her interest in learning and was mentally alert and interested until her death at 96 years of age.

Mother was very happy with her church relationship. She attended Sunday school all her life and was proud to be a member of the Fidelis Agape Sunday School Class until most of the members were passed and they had to join a younger class. She was a loyal member of the Women's Mission Group of the First Baptist Church. She left her list of favorite songs with us as "Great is Thy Faithfulness", "I Walked Today Where Jesus Walked, and her Mother's favorite, "Love Lifted Me". Her favorite Bible verse was Philippians Chapter 4, Verse 4-9 and the 121st Psalm.

Dad was active in the First Baptist Church of Gainesville and was great friends with the pastors. He especially liked Franklin Owens and Warner Fusselle during their times there. He designed the podium for the Church and several renovations throughout the years. He designed a Pastorium for Dr. Fusselle, but after he leftthe next Pastor did not want to live there. The Pastor's salary had risen to the point that Pastors could use the living stipend to buy their own house. The Church sold the Pastorium. Our original Church was downtown on Green Street. It was Marble on the outside with Georgian columns. During Dr. Fusselle's pastorate it burned and the Church rebuilt a much larger one further up Green Street where it sits in splendor today. Dad also performed design jobs for that new Church.

Dad became a noted designer of Churches in the region. He was close friends with many Pastors and designed additions or entire churches during his career after leaving Carroll Daniel Construction Company.

Fig. 92 Chicopee First Baptist Church

Fig. 93 Sanctuary

LAW OFFICES: NORTON, SMITH & MAJORS
380 GREEN STREET, N.E.
GAINESVILLE, GEORGIA

Fig 94. *Dad and Bill Norton became great friends*

JACK BUTTERWORTH SITS IN FRONT OF HUGE MURAL AT GAINESVILLE TEEN CE...
... Has Been in the Business a Long Time

The Man Behind the Mural

By ED KIDD
Times Staff Writer

...contains orange, blue, yellow, red — 11 erent colors — in rectangles, ares, ovals, triangles and a iety of other shapes — 204 t of abstract, but not chedelic, mural. The Gainesville Teen Center's ... is the work of several

...along with the natural wood trimmings and valances, provides a subdued contrast to the bright mural.

"Blinking star lighting is what the lighting experts call it," Jack said of the galaxy of small star-shaped lights in the ceiling of the room. The ceiling is painted a night sky color, almost black, that, with the tiny ...

...but out of doors.

The center will be able to accommodate as many as 350 people at one time. Booths will line the three walls under the mural. A 20-ton air-conditioning unit will provide both cooling and heating.

Bert T. Millard, architect, with whom Butterworth is associated, did much of the planning of the center. Butter-

...third year at Mercer law school. Mrs. Butterworth teaches at Enota Elementary School.

The Butterworths are members of the First Baptist Church, and Jack designed the pastorium.

"My primary concern choosing designs for a is that the customer like it. Jack said. One might envy

Fig. 95 Jack Butterworth designs the Youth Center

Gainesville Civic Center

At the time of my High School graduation and move to Emory University in Atlanta, the family moved next door into Mr. Bill Hood's former house, 301 North Avenue, N.E.

Fig. 96 301 North Avenue

Fig. 97 Patio

The Hoods moved into Chattahoochee Estates near Lake Lanier and the Country Club. Dad designed their house and Billy's too as I remember. There are many homes in Chattahoochee Estates that Dad designed over the years. We took some pictures to make an album of his work but it was never completed. We still have boxes of his designs in storage.

Our new house was home for Mom and Pop as they were called by their grandchildren until their death. They enjoyed the house as did we. They rented out the basement for several years to Lou Sarah McConnell, a friend of Mother's and a fellow teacher. A garage apartment was also rented and these incomes supplemented their retirement income. Jim and I had rooms on the second floor and they were on the main floor. Many a family and friend were entertained in that house from 1956 until 1997.

Fig. 98 Dining Room

Fig. 99 Living Room with Big Mama's Sofa displayed

Fig. 100 Guest Bedroom and Gertrude's room her last months

The front porch was screened and made a good evening retreat for talks and visits. The back yard was a garden spot for Gertrude who tended a wonderful flower array in addition to a pomegranate tree imported from Vienna and tomato plants. Myron Bennett was the last tenant in the garage apartment and after Mother died, he purchased the house and updated it to modern standards. Myron was a good friend of Mother after Dad's death and maintained the yard as part of his rent fee.

Jim graduated Gainesville High and left for North Georgia College in 1960. After graduation he attended Law School at Mercer in Macon, Ga. He practiced for a time in Macon then he moved to Cornelia Georgia. He practices there in addition to having a Judgeship in Habersham County today. He and Sandra Brown married and their children are James Blakely and Catherine Boen (Nutting).

Fig. 101 Boen and Mike Nutting

Jimmy flies for Delta and is a Georgia State Senator. Boen lives in Mooresville NC and is Principal of her Elementary School. Jim is now married happily to Rhonda Zimmerman and they live on Mud Creek Road in Habersham County, Georgia.

Fig. 102 Blake, John, and Jimmy Butterworth

I graduated Emory and attended the Medical College of Georgia in Augusta Georgia. After graduation in 1964, I interned in Asheville NC at Memorial Mission Hospital. After that Internship I joined the Army and took basic training at Fort Sam Houston in San Antonio TX where my first son, John, was born

Fig. 103 John and Evans Butterworth

I married Linda Helton of Gainesville and my first son John Virgil was born at Ft. Sam Houston. We were later stationed with the 6th Special Forces Group at Fort Bragg NC. This was during the Vietnam War and I was sent back to Augusta and Ft. Gordon following a jungle training course to prepare for a ship ride to Vietnam. With the 29th Civil Affairs Company, I went to Danang Vietnam and then Quang Ngai for a year. On return I went back to Augusta for General Surgery and Urology residencies. In 1971 I completed training and joined a Urology group in Bristol TN. Linda and I were divorced in 1985.

Fig. 104 Bristol's Own Dixieland Jazz Band

Bristol avocation as Trombone man in Bristol's Own Dixieland Jazz Band- A holdover from Mr. Donald Rich's assigning me the instrument in the 5th Grade Candler Street School. Logo design by Jack Butterworth, Sr.

I married **Nancy Colleen Godsey** on 15 February, 1988.

Nancy has a daughter, **Amanda Grace** who became a part of our family upon our marriage accepting our name- Amanda Grace Butterworth. She graduated Tennessee High School, Vanderbilt University with a major in Philosophy, and King College where she received her MBA. She was the Director of Admissions at King College for several years and now represents Allergan Pharmaceuticals. She lives in Knoxville, TN. Amanda is a gifted pianist, a Queen of Hearts in Bristol, and active in Junior Legague, Young Knoxville Professionals, and Fellowship Church in Knoxville, TN.

Fig. 105 Amanda Grace Butterworth

Fig. 106 John, Evans, Jack, Amanda, aaand Nancy 2007

Fig. 107 Nancy and Bobby

Nancy is a Bristol native and graduated from Tennessee High School. She trained as a Licensed Practical Nurse and became a Urology Nurse at Bristol Urological. She was Office Manager for many years and then attended Tri State Nursing College in Abingdon, Virginia followed by enrollment at King College in Bristol graduating Summa Cum Laude with a Bachelors Degree in Nursing. She currently works as an emergency department nurse at Bristol Regional Hospital.

Fig. 108 Nancy Coleen Godsey Butterworth

I retired from Bristol Urological Associates in 2004 only to join the hospital as VP of Medical Affairs

Fig. 109 Butterworths

for five more years. I retired from that position in July 2010. My second son, Evans, was born in Bristol in 1976. **John Virgil Butterworth** married **Jamie McGuire** whom he met while a student at Emory. Jamie worked for several years with Chick-fil-A as the rare woman executive. She currently is an active mother of two daughters and has contributed to the family movie productions. She was a member of the Emory Chorus and is a talented singer.

Fig. 110 John & Jamie Butterworth

Both John and Jamie are Emory Alums. John was with Disney for 15 years and now is with Verizon Digital Media Services. John, a very athletic and musically talented young man, has become a devoted father to his daughters. He rebuilt a VW based Dune Buggy from the ground up using only a book as an instructor. He formed his own rock band to include his friends, wife, and daughters. Jamie, Sarah and Rebecca starred in a feature film in 2008 called Summer Eleven which was shown internationally in several film festivals including the Heartland Film Festival in Indiana.

John and Jamie with friends in the entertainment business wrote and filmed a children's version of A Mid Summer Night's Dream which was shown in the National Movie Festival in Idaho in 2010.

They have two daughters, Sarah and Rebecca and live in Burbank California.

Fig. 111 Sarah Elizabeth Butterworth

Fig. 112 Rebecca Clark Butterworth

William Evans Butterworth, my second son graduated from Tennessee High in Bristol as did John and Mandy. He was an Eagle Scout in Troop 3, First Presbyterian Church. He attended and graduated from Furman University in Greenville, SC with a degree in Drama and minor in French. He spent one season in France and toured England and Scotland. He is now with Warner Brothers Studios after terms with Technicolor, Todd AO, and several other movie production companies. He has written, directed, and filmed his own movie, The Carbon Copy, and thoroughly enjoys working in the entertainment industry.

Fig. 113 William Evans Butterworth

Jackson Evans Butterworth Sr. had a sudden and unexpected stroke on 29 August 1989. Until that time he continued to visit, entertain, and work at his drafting table with good mental acuity and pleasant affect. His major joy was his wife Gertrude and his family. He was hospitalized but could not be sustained without life support. He is buried in Gainesville at the Alta Vista Cemetery.

Fig. 114 Jackson Evans Butterworth, Sr.

Gertrude Annette Newby Butterworth lived a long life and was mentally vigorous until the end of life.

Fig. 115 Gertrude Newby Butterworth

She was severely burdened with osteoporosis for the last decade. She sustained multiple fractures, many unrecognized. She underwent bilateral hip surgery as well as long periods of rehabilitation and medical treatment for this disorder. During all of her life she continued to exhibit a sense of humor and sincere interest in her family and friend's concerns. A fall was her terminal event when she hit her head on a night table sustaining a subdural hematoma from which she never recovered. She was pronounced dead on August 5, 2007. She would have been 96 years old the following December 1, 2007. Until her fall she was interested in her family, church, and friends. Her mental ability was still youthful with humor and interest abounding. Her body simply could not keep up with her mind. She is buried alongside Jack in Alta Vista Cemetery

Life Accomplishments

Jack and Gertrude represented an example of an ideal marriage for their times. They showed persistent love for each other and joy in their relationship. Eachgave unselfishly to their children and devoted their time and resources to them. This was in the manner of their upbringing and the community which they knew. Together, they viewed honesty, integrity, and a "good name" as a higher value than the accumulation of material wealth. They believed in the value and reward education and steered their children in that path. Their belief in family was clan-like in loyalty. This was the example shown to each of their sons during their formative years. Gert nurtured and guided her sons when some would have said it was excessive. Such action embodied her core belief and she held on to those values her entire life. At her funeral, there was a large gathering present to celebrate her life and to remember her spirit and contributions to others. The elderly often do not have such an attendance as their peers have gone ahead. Her role in the lives of her community and the children she taught was evident in the response to her passing.

Tribute to Values

Societal changes have tried to devalue the values outlined in the stories of the Butterworth and Newby families. Those values are less typical in the 21st century American life than they were in the historical "snap shot" of 1908-2007. The "nuclear" family has declined in degree as the primary family style compared to the time of Gert and Jack Butterworth. Society is moving toward the broader perspectives of multiculturalism, international government, political correctness, social humanism, and more intellectually accepted themes.

All families have a story to tell and often with great pride and affection. This one is not unique to its time. However, I believe we can benefit from such reviews and reassessing our values to assure ourselves that we are achieving joy and satisfaction from our God given life.We often find comfort and reassurance in the myth of Camelot and in the persistent morality of Billy Graham's teachings and his life's example. Jack and Gert's story is one other such chronicle which can be molded into a treasure and model for us to emulate as we journey into the turbulent future.

Fig. 116 The Butterworths in Orange County California,
2005 Front Row L to R: Sarah, Gertrude, Rebecca; Back Row L to R:
Jim, Jack, John, Evans, Boen Butterworth Nutting, Jimmy

Appendix

I. Origin of the Butterworth name:

A. Viking Origin

There are several versions of the Origin of the Butterworth name and family. This first is one citing a **Norse** origin which could well be valid and predate any subsequent story.

A. Wm. Robinson, in "The Social and Political History of Rochdale, says that "this surname used to be pronounced BUTTEROTH, locally."

The grandson of Charles Butterworth, of Town Meadows, Commander Henry Butterworth, R.N. has kindly supplied, Feb., 1926, from recollections of over a quarter of a century ago the following account, communicated to him in 1890, by his friend, the late Adm. Sir Clements Markham, K.C.B., F.R.S., P/R.G.S., d.1916, and obtained by the Admiral at the end of 1899, from a member of the Athenaeum Club, "interested in pedigrees and the derivation of names."

The etymology suggested was as follows;

"The name Butterworth is derived from BUTER WOHL", the home or house , of BUTER, who appears to have been a Norse Viking, who joined Harold Haarfarger in his rebellion against his brother Harold Haardraade. The rebellion proved abortive, and Harold Haafaarger was defeated and killed in a sea action off the Orkneys or Shetlands. His fleet was dispersed, and after great trials at sea, Buter sailed down the West Coast of Scotland, but was prevented from landing through "the inhospitable nature of the coast, and the ferocity of the inhabitants." Buter finally landed in Morcambe Bay Lancashire, and presumably from there worked his way inland."

This account, together with some record of the Butterworth family history, by the Member of the Athenaeum Club, was given by Admiral Sir Clements Markham to Commander Henry Butterworth, who, sailing for Australia soon after April 1890, lost this and all his possessions when the "Dacca" was wrecked on the Daedalus Rock, in the Red Sea.

If these two Harolds, described as "brothers", Harold Haarfaager and Harold Haardraade, are meant to be identical with the famous Norwegian Kings, there would appear to be considerable confusion, chronologically, in the narrative here. Of the Kings of Norway, Harold I, Harold Harfagr, or Haafager (Fair Haired), b. A.D.850; reigned 1046-66; invaded England with Tostig, the outlawed brother of Harold II., King of the English, son of Godwin, Earl of Kent, who defeated and slew them at **Stamford** Bridge,25 Sept., 1066. Harold of England being himself defeated and slain 19 days later 14 Oct., 1066, at the Battle of Hastings, or Senlac by William the Conqueror.

Apart from the identification of the two Harolds with whom Buter is here linked, the suggested etymology for the name Butterworth may have solid foundation. As an alternative theory, I offer the following, based on the derivations of the two words BUTTER, and WORTH, given in "The

Romance of Names", 3rd edition,1922,by Prof. Ernest Weekley, M.A., though neither in this, nor in his "Surnames",1st ed. 1916, does the complete name BUTTERWORTH appear.

In "The Romance of Names", however, the surname BUTTERFIELD is mentioned, as derived from BITTERN-FIELD. From:-The Romance of Names, pp.220, 123, & 117: "BUTTER", French BUTER,"a bittor", in Colgrave`s French-English Dict. of 1911, is a dialect name for the "bittern", called a Butter-bump, by Tennyson`s "Northern Farmer", line 31.

"WORTH" was perhaps originally applied to land by a river, or a holm; in the North, a river island was commonly called HOLM, from the Scandinavian, also pronounced HOME, HULME,and HUME, e.g. in compounds confused with -ham, e.g. DURHAM, which was once DUN-HOLMR, hill-island.

According to this view, the surname, like so many others, is derived from a place-name, BUTTER-WORTH meaning "land by the river, or river island, frequented by the bittern," a marsh-loving bird allied to the heron, having a booming note, from which characteristics, indeed, the Norse Viking, Buter, may perhaps have been named or nick-named.

Families migrating from this locality would describe themselves as de BOTER-, or de BUTER-WORTH, de BUTTERWORTH, and so ultimately, BUTTERWORTH.

The first mentioned derivation, according to which Butterworth means "BUTER`S land by the river, or river island," is not, quite possibly the more correct etymology, but further investigation is desirable confirming the existence and career of this Norse Viking, and the approximate date of his landing in Lancashire.

A list of place names, beginning with BUTE-, BUTTE-, or BUTER-, with the suggestive terminal syllables,-leigh, or -ley or -ly, -mere, -side,-wick, etc, to be met with in the North and South of Great Britain, most, if not all of which would appear to derive from their having been haunts of the bittern has been listed. Their number and widespread distribution favor the conclusions that the name Butterworth originated in a place-name, and means BITTERN-, not BUTER'S-LAND.

B. David Butterworth Version

The second derivation is a version identified by David Butterworth of England who corresponded with me many times during his research in the 1990s. W. Evans Butterworth, b. 1976, visited and spent time in the village of residence with David during his trip to England in the 1990s. David lived last in the Lake Country of Middle England at Bay Cottage, Milburn, Penrith in 1995. He wrote that he was the Milburn village Treasurer of Village Hall, Secretary to the Entertainment Committee and on the Flower Committee as well as the historian of Milburn during his retirement. He did considerable research on the Butterworth family and much credit is due him for this study. He included the Charles Ball book in his analysis of Butterworths. David once said he thought all Butterworths were related at some juncture. He unfortunately was unable to identify definitely the home and birth site of our Isaac Butterworth who migrated to Maryland in the late 17th cn.

Fig. 117 Milburn, Penrith, England 1995. Retirement Village of David Butterworth

NOTES

ON

SOME FAMILIES

OF

BUTTERWORTH

- The founder of the Butterworth family was a certain Reginald (Reynald, Reinaud) who lived in the time of King Stephen (1135-1154).{ Almost a century after Buter sailed with Harold} His son Gilbert owed 40 shillings to the Exchequer in 1184 for having recognition of his right to land in Butterworth (correctly Boterworth - the farmstead of Boter) and Peselton. Butterworth itself lay to the south east of Rochdale, Lancashire and gave its name, not only to the family, but also to a township in the Parish of Rochdale. Gilbert's great grandson Geoffrey de Boterworth (this spelling persisted until Tudor times) sold Butterworth to Sir John and Dame Joan de Byron about 1270 and representation of the family passed to Geoffrey's second cousin, Roger. Roger's descendants became established as gentry at Belfield Hall, also in the Township of Butterworth, and remained there until the direct line failed with the death of Alexander VI in 1728, when Belfield passed to strangers in blood. It was pulled down in 1914. Two junior branches of the Butterworths of Belfield survive to this day, to one of which belonged Major General William John Butterworth (1801-1856), Governor of Singapore, after whom the town of Butterworth in Malaysia was named. A second gentry family Jived at The Holt about a mile from Belfield from before 1400 to 1559.

- A second major branch of the family descends from Henry Butterworth (1702-1785), a blacksmith in Rossendale, Lancashire. Four of his sons became Baptist Ministers and his descendants include Joseph Butterworth MP (1770-1826) who played an important part in the abolition of the Slave Trade, Henry (1786-1860) who founded the eminent firm of legal and medical publishers, and George (1885-1916) the composer. They are usually referred to as the Butterworth's of Coventry because of their 90 year sojourn in that city.

- There were also several families of yeoman farmers. Two, the Butterworths of Lowhouse and Wildhouse, had a recognized descent from Roger de Boterworth above, becoming extinct in their direct lines in the seventeenth century. Most of the others only appear in documents for the first time in the sixteenth century and all had ceased to be yeoman farmers by the middle of the eighteenth century. It has been possible to trace only one of these families down to the twentieth century. An old established American family is covered and in addition there is an Addendum of individuals of note whom it has not been possible to connect to any of the above branches.

- Rochdale St Chad records start in 1582, but although Milnrow Chapel was founded in 1496 the baptismal records start only in 1726 with burials only from 1799. The lack of early records may be due to a flood in 1723 that caused much damage and may account for the apparent lack of some baptismal records.

- In order to give some idea of the value of rents, bequests etc. in earlier years I have included a modem estimated value in brackets after the original figure - the factors used are given in Appendix 2. These relate to the purchase of goods. Real wages have risen approximately five-fold since 1900 and ten-fold since 1800, so the £8,000 pounds with which Thomas Butterworth, 1684-1745, endowed his daughter Susanna (see ChlO No 8) would be worth about £ 1million now for buying goods, but at least £5 million now for purchasing labour. If one allows for income tax then the £5 million becomes about £8 million.

- The pedigree of each family is broken down into one or more detailed charts giving all persons including husbands and wives together with dates in full. Each chart is followed by a list of sources, a general note if relevant and biographical notes on each member of the family giving whatever information is available. The biographical notes, which do not necessarily include everybody, are organized by generation moving from left to right.

Table of Contents of David Butterworth's Book

- **Alexander IV 2-9** Alexander extended, or even totally rebuilt, Belfield round a courtyard about 45 feet square, with two splendid rooms in the north wing: on the ground floor a grand new dining room nearly 40 feet long and above it an equally grand great chamber of the same size, both rooms being fitted with enormous south facing windows filled with glass which was then very expensive.

- In his will it is clear that Alexander, who, although he was a country gentleman, was of relatively modest means, had seriously over-extended himself: there was no extra money for his widow, wood had to be sold to pay his debts and more debts were to be incurred to give the younger children a very modest portion. In addition the inventory of contents makes no mention of any silverware - a surprising omission. (In the 1670's a gang in Westmorland made a specialty of stealing silver (and only silver) from isolated farmhouses).

- It is clear that Alexander wanted to create an image of himself and his family that was beyond his means: in modern terms he was like the man who reckons his lifestyle needs an expensive BMW (bought on credit) rather than the Ford Mondeo he can really afford.

- **William 2-21** It is clear that William spent the money that he had personally borrowed, hence the need for a mortgage on the Cheshire estate in 1662, but on what is not known. A possibility is that he was intending to buy a Baronetcy.

- On his return to England in 1660 Charles II proceeded to create an enormous number of Baronetcies (over 200 by the end of 1661). The majority went to Cavalier families who had helped Charles in exile or to recover his crown. Unfortunately, William, who was clearly proud of his family (c.f. the entail) didn't qualify on either count.

- In 1647 Charles I granted 2 blank patents for Scottish Baronetcies to Sir Robert Carr of Etal in Northumberland. On 8 Aug 1661, 2 months after William's death, Charles II allowed their renewal. If William had secretly negotiated and paid for a title, Carr would have had a real temptation to pocket the money and say nothing! A Baronetcy would have moved William from being one amongst about 8,000 gentry to one in the top *400/500* families: very important in a hierarchical society.

- **Nathaniel IV** 4-2 Despite extensive research it has not proved possible to find him in the 1861 Census in Oldham, Crompton, Chadderton, Middleton, Royton, Hopwood, Pilsworth, Castleton or Butterworth, nor to trace his burial or any children.

- **Stuart Colin 25-14** Add: His degree was a 2.1 in Film &Video and in Jan 1998 he joined (on contract) the Consumer Affairs Dept of the BBC working as a researcher on "Watchdog".

- **Chart 26** Mary Josephine to Alfred Edward are the children of Joseph Henry and Mary Eliza Alexandrina : the vertical line joining them has been omitted.

Relative to Coats of Arms, David found that there were two general Coats of Arms and three specifics. The last three have been specifically granted to people in the last 200 years.

Specific:

1. 17 Feb. 1816 to Joseph, M.P., eagles and lions and chevron
2. 15 Nov. 1855 to General Butterworth, a modified general coat of arms.
3. 15 May 1985 to Lord Butterworth when he was made a peer.
4. No one can use these unless descended from these families.

II. The General Coats of Arms

1. The blue lion, red coronet on a silver shield held since at least 1383/4 by the main line of the family-i.e. like Butterworths of Belfield and their descendants.
2. Sable, a cross engrailed between 4 plumbs argent. The background is black, the cross white, and the plums are white(silver)

This appears in Burkes General Armory with crest: a sphere resting on a cloud proper. The College and Arms tracked it back to 1599 and concluded it was used during the 15th and 16th centuries but did not know by whom. They also said the Crest was probably 19th century. This meant the Butterworths had a Second gentry family –but whom?

"I have found 9 yeoman families but none were rich enough to be gentry. Then I remembered Butterworth of the Holt. There was so little I hadn't bothered with them, but when I dug out all the references and 'bingo', in 1559 they had 800 acres-as many as in the Belfield family."

"You will be descended from one or the other families, Belfield or the Holt, so take your choice- I recommend the plums-no one else is using it as far as I know and it would be nice to know it is in use again. The reason the College of Arms didn't know whose it was because the Holt family died out in the main line in 1559 before the list was made in 1599. It should also be easier to engrave on a signet ring that the lion and coronets. Cheers, David."

Sable, a cross

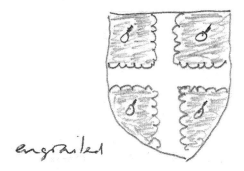

engrailed

between 4 plumbs argent.

Fig. 118 Belfield Butterworth Coat of Arms

Fig. 119 Newby Coat of Arms

C. Newby Coat of Arms / Newby Family Crest

The surname of NEWBY was a locational name of 'Newby' a township in the union of Ripon, Yorkshire. Local names usually denoted where a man held land. Early records of the name mention Nicholas de Neuby 1273 County Yorkshire. Local surnames, by far the largest group, derived from a place name where the man held land or from the place from which he had come, or where he actually lived. These local surnames were originally preceded by a preposition such as "de", "atte", "by" or "in". The names may derive from a manor held, from working in a religious dwelling or from literally living by a wood or marsh or by a stream. Following the Crusades in Europe a need was felt for a family name. This was recognized by those of noble blood, who realized the prestige and practical advantage it would add to their status. Other records mention Galfridus de Nuby of Yorkshire was listed in the Yorkshire Poll Tax of 1379. Radulphus de Neuby 1379 ibid. The associated arms are recorded in Sir Bernard Burkes General Armory registered during the time of Richard 11 (1377-1399) to John de Newby. The origin of badges and emblems, are traced to the earliest times, although, Heraldry, in fact, cannot be traced later than the 12th century, or at furthest the 11th century. At first armorial bearings were probably like surnames and assumed by each warrior at his free will and pleasure, his object being to distinguish himself from others. It has long been a matter of doubt when bearing Coats of Arms first became hereditary. It is known that in the reign of Henry V (1413-1422), a proclamation was issued, prohibiting the use of heraldic ensigns to all who could not show an original and valid right, except those 'who had borne arms at Agincourt'. The College of Arms (founded in 1483) is the Royal corporation of heralds who record proved pedigrees and grant armorial bearings.

III. The 31st Alabama Infantry Regiment

Brief History

The 31st Alabama Infantry Regiment was organized at Talladega, 16 March 1862, with men from Calhoun, Cherokee, Montgomery, Randolph, Shelby, and Talladega counties. It reported to Gen'l Danville Leadbetter at Chattanooga shortly after. It then moved up to Knoxville, where it was brigaded under Gen'l Seth Barton, in Carter Stevenson's Division. The regiment was at the investment of Cumberland Gap, and it took part in the fight at Tazewell. With Gen'l E. K. Smith's column, it was in the Kentucky Campaign, without coming up with the enemy. When the forces came back, it was permanently brigaded with the 20th, 23rd, 30th, and 46th Alabama regiments, under Gen'l Edward D. Tracy of Madison, Department of Mississippi and East Louisiana. In December, the 31st accompanied Stevenson's Division to Vicksburg. In May 1863 it helped defend Port Gibson, Mississippi, where the regiment suffered severely. It fought at Baker's Creek, and the loss was heavy. As part of the Vicksburg garrison, the regiment suffered through the siege, and after losing a number killed and wounded, it was surrendered with the fortress. Placed in parole camp at Demopolis, the 31st was soon exchanged. With Gen'l Edmund Pettus in command of the brigade, the regiment joined the Army of Tennessee, and it was engaged with slight loss at Mission Ridge. It wintered at Dalton, and it participated in the campaign from Dalton to Atlanta. The regiment followed Gen'l John Bell Hood into Tennessee and sustained severe losses at Columbia and Nashville, and was the rear-guard of the retreating army. Transferred to North Carolina, the regiment was hotly engaged at Bentonville, and a fragment of the 1100 with which it entered the service surrendered at Greensboro, as part of Pettus' Brigade. There were 260 effectives in January, 1863, with 21 k and 37 w at Vicksburg. There were 23 casualties at Chattanooga, and in December, 1863, there were 452 present with 323 arms. Only 180 were fit for duty in January 1865, and less than 100 surrendered in April. Toward the close of the war, the 31st was consolidated with the 23rd and 46th Infantry and redesignated the 23rd Consolidated Infantry Regiment at Smithfield, 9 April 1865.

IV. Butterworth Land in Virginia 1740+

Benjamin Butterworth patented land on Sycamore Creek, on Staunton River, and later made his home there in 1748. He lived in Amelia County, Virginia and sold the plantation in 1748 when he moved to the Staunton River land. This is the land visited by Jack and Jim Butterworth in 2009 and depicted in the body of the story. This was slightly downriver from Clement Hill the home of Benjamin's wife Elizabeth Clement and her family. Benjamin's son Stephen also married a Clement, Rachel, who was likely a cousin and daughter of Elizabeth's brother Isaac Clement. On visiting the land site one can clearly see how close the inhabitants of the frontier could be to each other using the river for transportation. The Staunton River at this site was a commercial avenue as planters took produce to market via rivers. The sites of the Butterworth and Clement holding were only a short distance by water. How one maneuvered upstream is unclear to modern men but it was likely polled or paddled against the strong current. So I conclude that courting by way of the river or perhaps horse was the practice.

When Halifax County became a county in 1751, Benjamin Clement, Gentleman and Father in Law of Benjamin Butterworth, was a Justice of the Peace and appointed Captain of a Company of Rangers for Halifax County Militia in 1755. He was one of the first to manufacture gunpowder in the Colony and he and his neighbor, Charles Lynch, had a Mill which turned out 50 pounds a day.

Benjamin's home is known as "Clement Hill", on a knoll overlooking the Staunton River, a mansion with corner fireplaces. He was a neighbor of Colonel John Lynch. Charles Clement, a son of Adam and Agnes Clement, inherited the place, and in 1803 married Nancy Hamby of Patrick and made his home there. They property passed to John L Hunt through a marriage with Nannie Clement, granddaughter of Charles and daughter of Charles, Jr.

The Virginia Gazette published in August 5, 1775 a letter from Mr. Charles Lynch: "Sometime ago my having made powder was mentioned in this paper..., I inform the public that Mr. Benjamin Clement is a partner with me in making the powder and that he was the first in the colony I have heard of who attempted to make it, although he did not bring it to perfection. Since our partnership, we have brought it so such perfection with salt-petre on our own making that the best riflemen approve of it; and with the little mill we now have, we can make 50 lbs a day. Salt-petre only is wanting, which may very easily be made by observing the following directions; and when it is considered how much we want powder and that salt-petre is the principal ingredient, it is hoped that those who have the good of their county at heart will exert themselves in making it. Without it, we can have no powder, consequently no means of defense; but with it we shall soon have booth in America, sir, your Humble Servant. Charles Lynch. August 5, 1775." The following directions for making salt-petre by digging up the dirt floors of old meat houses, boiling the soil and straining the liquor through straw in the process somewhat similar to making lye from wood ashes."

V. McCollum's Brigade of Rangers Georgia Militia

The August issue of *The Crescent Chronicle* carried a lead article about a student project to mark the historic grave of Aaron Burris, a Cherokee, Georgia county resident who died between January and April 1864, a victim of the Home Guard. The article accurately described the last year of the Civil War in North Georgia as one of Cherokee County's darkest chapters. It also characterized the Home Guard as an unofficial band and as one of the lesser known evils of the war. My purpose (author of article) in writing this article is to put the Home Guard into historical perspective and to offer a short biography of Benjamin Franklin McCollum, its leader in Cherokee and Pickens Counties. This is a very personal story of a life interrupted by war and cut short by violence.

Benjamin Franklin McCollum was born November 9. 1843 in Walton County, Georgia. He was the fifth child (and fifth son) of Jesse Miller McCollum (1811-1907) and his first wife, Elizabeth A. Edwards (18181853), who were born in South Carolina. Jesse's father, William (17891876), served in the War of 1812 in South Carolina, and his grandfather, Daniel (1760-1850), served in the Revolution in North Carolina. This line of McCollum's was founded in America by **John N. McCollum (1658-1760), a Scot who was banished "to the King's plantations abroad" on July 31, 1685 for his role in a rebellion.** John was transported to the colony of New Jersey aboard the *Henry and Francis of Newcastle* and settled in Somerset County. He became an elder of the Basking Ridge Presbyterian Church, in whose cemetery his body rests.

After the Revolution Daniel McCollum moved from Rowan County North Carolina to the Pendleton District of South Carolina, where he remained until February 1826, when he moved to Habersham County, Georgia. He lived in the Blue Creek District of that county until his death in 1850. He is buried in the Old Blue Creek Baptist Church Cemetery in an area that became White County in 1857. His previously unmarked grave was marked with a tombstone commemorating his Revolutionary War service on July 4, 2002.

William "Billy" McCollum married his first wife, Susannah Miller (1788-1824) in South Carolina on June 10, 1810 and their son, Jesse, was born the next year. Billy left South Carolina for Habersham County Georgia in 1823, three years before his father. Susannah died in 1824 and was the first person buried at the Old Blue Creek Baptist Church Cemetery. Billy remarried on September 28, 1826 to Esther H. Edwards and the family remained in Habersham County until after 1830, when they moved to Walton County.

Jesse married in Walton County in 1833 and lived there until after 1840. His family was in Cobb County in 1850 and was enumerated in the July 9, 1860 census of Cherokee County in the Wildcat District.

Benjamin was shown as 17 years old in that census, although he would not turn 17 until November. When the Civil War broke out, about a dozen Cherokee County Mc Collums including Benjamin enlisted in Georgia volunteer infantry and cavalry units that would serve in both the Army of Northern Virginia and the Army of Tennessee. Benjamin enlisted on April 18, 1861 in Company F of the 2nd Regiment, Georgia Volunteer Infantry for a term of one year marked by several illnesses including camp fever, which hospitalized him. The last entry in his compiled service record with the 2nd Regiment was on May 22, 1862 when he was returned to duty with his unit after a stay in Chimborazo Hospital Number 5 in Richmond, Virginia. His one year enlistment expired while he was in the hospital, so he was probably discharged from service and returned home.

His service record picks up again on August 6, 1862 when he took his own horse to Richmond Virginia and enlisted in Company C (Cherokee Dragoons) of the Phillips Legion Cavalry for "three years or the war." In March 1863 General Robert E. Lee assigned the Phillips Legion Cavalry to the Cavalry Corps of the Army of Northern Virginia, under the command of General J.E.B. Stuart. It served in that army until the final winter of the war.

Benjamin appeared on muster rolls and pay records throughout 1863, but there is little specific information about his activities. During that period the Legion was involved in several significant battles, including Chancellorsville and Gettysburg. A notation in his record shows that from July 19 to September 30, 1863 he served as a courier. Another indicates that his horse was valued at $1300.00. A muster roll for the period during which Aaron Burris was killed in Cherokee County, shows that Benjamin was with his unit in Virginia from December 31 1863 until April 24, 1864. He was then shown on furlough until August 15, 1864. Company muster rolls taken on the last day of September and the last day of October 1864 show him as absent without leave (AWOL) since August 16, 1864.

The North Georgia that Benjamin came home to was not the one he left in 1862. His older brothers John and George had been killed in the war. His younger brother, Robert, who served with him in Company C from February 1864, was wounded on June 11, 1864 and was sent home for 60 days to recuperate. Quite possibly Benjamin accompanied him. Robert, too, was shown on the muster roll as

AWOL after August 6, 1864. His uncle, Enoch, an infantry company commander, had died of measles with his unit in Tennessee. And his cousin, Moses, also died of disease in Tennessee leaving a young pregnant widow and a two year old daughter.

The record is not conclusive, but it does not appear that Benjamin ever returned to the Army of Northern Virginia. He seems, though, to have had official status in his Home Guard activities in North Georgiaas attested to by a September 5, 1864 commission from Governor Joseph E. Brown making him a Captain in the Blackhorse Cavalry of the Georgia State Militia. On November 26 of that year acting Brigadier General Jesse A. Glenn issued Special Orders No. 16 authorizing Colonel B.F. McCollum to raise and organize a regiment for his "Brigade of Cavalry of Reserves and non-conscripts." According to the latter document the companies McCollum organized were to be part of Glenn's Cavalry, headquartered at Athens Georgia and their muster rolls were to be forwarded to the Adjutant and Inspector General's office in Richmond. In an inspection report sent to Major General Howell Cobb at the end of January 1865, "Colonel McCollum" was reported to be in Canton with 100 men. The inspector was concerned that the Home Guard was not operating as a unit and recommended that all of them be mustered as soon as possible and sent as a fighting unit to General Lee. It is doubtful that Governor Brown would have approved such a move, but it apparently never took place. Benjamin McCollum's Home Guard unit was known in Cherokee County as "McCollum's Scouts." Some histories of Cherokee and Pickens Counties written in the early 20th century portray him as a deserter and renegade leader of an outlaw band that preyed ruthlessly on the citizens of North Georgia. At the time of his Home Guard activities, General Sherman had invaded and occupied much of Georgia, leaving behind a swath of destruction and troops to protect the railroad, which was his vital supply and communications line. That railroad passed through Cherokee and Pickens Counties and the "Scouts" found it and foraging Union troops to be good targets.

Sherman's attitude about his Southern adversaries was contained in a letter he wrote in September 1863 while camped at Big Black, Mississippi. He was responding to a question from President Lincoln's military advisor about the nature of the Southern people and the type of government that would have to be set up in occupied areas. Sherman divided the Southern population into four classes: the large planters, the small farmers, the pro-Union segment and the "young bloods." The first three classes he believed could be controlled by an occupation government, but the "young bloods" were the flaming youth of the Confederacy, the hard-riding, quick-shooting young men of good family who followed leaders like Jeb Stuart and Nathan Bedford Forrest and gave the Southern army a cavalry that Sherman frankly admired. These men Sherman regarded as "dangerous subjects in every sense." If no way could be found to harness and redirect their violent, disruptive inclinations, "this class of men must all be killed."

Benjamin Franklin McCollum was a "young blood" and he had a reputation by the time the war ended. The Reconstruction years were difficult for him and for his family.

He had married Roseanna (Rosey) Lucinda Garrison on January 17, 1865 and came home in April after the surrender at Appomattox to start a family. In the five years following the war he and Rosey had three daughters. In 1876 they had a son. He ran a blacksmith shop in Canton until at least 1870. In the 1870s he read law and set up a private practice in Brooks Station, Fayette County, Georgia. His calling card said that he would practice in the Clayton, Fayette, Coweta, Pike, Meriwether and Spalding Superior Courts and the Supreme Court.

A few glimpses into Benjamin's life in the 1870s appeared in *Atlanta Constitution* articles. The May 24, 1873 edition of the paper reported an attempt by a posse from Pickens County to arrest him at his home in Canton on a murder charge stemming from an incident during the Civil War. The state legislature had stricken the indictment from the docket, but it had recently been revived and the group of a dozen armed men intended to take him "dead or alive." He succeeded in escaping from them by slashing their leader with a knife and eluding a volley of gunfire. The February 2, 1877 edition of the paper reported that there was to be a Sheriff's sale of land, a dwelling and a storehouse belonging to B.F. McCollum in Fayette County to satisfy a tax lien. On October 27, 1877 the paper reported that Brooks Station had been awakened a few days before by a "regular war" between three Brassell brothers and Benjamin McCollum in which pistols were used until Benjamin got the better of one of the brothers in a "rough and tumble tussle." On January 8, 1879 Benjamin got into an altercation in Brooks Station with another attorney, Reverend John G. Caldwell and "knocked him senseless." A follow-up article in the January 16th issue of the paper noted, "Mr. Caldwell's friends think he was unjustifiably attacked and Colonel McCollum's friends claim that he was justifiable in the attack."

By 1880 he had moved to Hampton in Henry County, where he continued his law practice. Apparently he made an enemy of the town's deputy marshal, Ben McKneely, who appears to have been running, or protecting, a brothel near Benjamin's office. The Daily Constitution of May 27, 28 and 29, 1880 recounted the story in detail. Several days before, Benjamin had complained to the town council that "a certain public closet was a nuisance" and asked that it be removed. When the council failed to act, he took it on himself to turn it over. McKneely put it back up and threatened to "kill any man who dared (to remove it)." He loaded a double barrel shotgun and placed it in a store near the closet. On May 26th two local men got into an argument about the closet, which escalated into a fight and gunfire. Benjamin intervened and took the pistol from one of the men and refused to turn it over the McKneely, who attempted to take it by force. Both men agreed to give it to the town marshal when he arrived on the scene. McCollum accused McKneely of drinking and McKneely called him a damned liar and the fight started again. McKneely left and came back with the shotgun, which he had placed in a nearby store earlier in the week. Several people prevented McKneely from shooting and one took the shotgun from him. Benjamin's friends urged him to leave, but he refused and words continued to be exchanged. McKneely grabbed the shotgun back and fired one barrel into Benjamin's chest and fired the second over his head as he fell to the ground dead.

Minutes later his family arrived to find him lying face down in the street in a pool of blood. The paper carried this graphic description of the scene:

"McCollum was hardly cold in death before his wife and four children heard the dreadful news. They rushed frantically to the scene and in the blood kneeled to cry in their passionate grief. The scene was one which moved strong men to tears, and added fresh horror to the tragedy."

The article concluded with the following descriptions of the two men:

"McCollum was a captain in the Confederate service and served with marked gallantry. He was known as a desperate man and had been more than once indicted for murder. He was about 40 years of age. McKneely is about 25. He is married and has two children. He is considered a dangerous man, and the common agreement seems to be that he had been drinking when the fatal affray occurred."

Benjamin was buried in Atlanta's Oakland Cemetery on May 28, 1880. He was 36 years old. Rosey Garrison remarried in 1891. In 1889 and 1890 she worked as a dressmaker in Atlanta. She died in 1934.

McKneely was never prosecuted for the murder. He escaped to Indian Territory (Oklahoma), where he lived out his life.

Postscript: A descendant of Ben's killer, Benjamin H. McNeely, provided a copy of a November 11, 1933 newspaper article from Talihina Oklahoma, which noted the 58th anniversary of Benjamin McNeely and his wife, who were married in Hampton, Georgia on November 12, 1875. They came to what had been called Rock Creek "five years after the Frisco Railroad came to the Rock Creek settlement changing its name to Talihina." Apparently, the murder he committed in Georgia never caught up with him.

VI. James Hughes 1758-1867

PIONEER HISTORY OF FORSYTH COUNTY, GEORGIA Chap. 24, p. 122

James Hughes came to America from Wales sometime before the Revolutionary War. The Family settled in Culpepper County, Virginia. He later migrated to Laurens County, South Carolina and married a woman named Gilbert, and had one child, a son, named Moses. James fought in the Revolutionary War and the War of 1812. He died in 1867 at the age of 109 and is buried near Alpharetta, Georgia.

VII. Hog Mountain, Georgia

The military fort erected near Hog Mountain was the result of the early settlement's being surrounded by Cherokee Indians who were at that time loyal to the British. The construction of Peachtree Road in

1813 made this community a center of trade and commercial activity. The Hog Mountain House was the first hotel in the county. It was erected by Shadrack Bogan, who married Ann Fee in Augusta and moved to Hog Mountain in 1815. Bogan also owned a store which was a trading post for whites and Indians. The Hog Mountain House was known for its hospitality, comfortable beds and good food.

Moore and Maltbie had been operating a trading post several years before Shadrack Bogan settled at Hog Mountain. Mr. Moore died in 1814 on a buying trip to New York, and Mr. Maltbie remained in the community and continued to run a prosper business until the county seat was moved in 1821. He became the first post master of Lawrenceville.

Hog Mountain has been in three different counties: Franklin, Jackson and Gwinnett. For many years it was on the stagecoach route. A mail route was authorized in 1821 from Monticello, Monroe, Lawrenceville, and on to Gainesville by way of Hog Mountain.

The Hog Mountain Baptist Church was organized in 1854 by Rev. Amos Hadaway and Rev. D.H. Moncrief. The charter members were Lucy Ann Pitman, Thomas Pitman, John M. Pitman, Frances M. Morgan, John Morgan, Amanda Pitman, Wm. T. Pitman, Julia Ann Head, Willis Head, Isabel Hadaway, and James R. Hadaway. The first building was erected in 1854 and replaced in 1905.

Sources:
History of Gwinnett County, 1818-1960, Volume II, by James C. Flanigan, copyright 1959

VIII. Newby Store

The general store in Vienna, Georgia was a prominent town establishment dating to the early 1900s. It was a gathering site as well as the source of clothing, novelties, and general merchandise. W.F. Newby began the institution and his sons, grandsons, and great grandsons carried it forward into the latter half of the century. The store served the town of Vienna as it offered delivery early in its existence. It served the county farmers as they came to "market" on weekends to replenish supplies. Ladies as well as men were offered clothing, cloth materials, as well as overalls and boots. The store is noted to have offered Pointer Brand overalls for decades. Newbys was a tradition as well as a business and was well known in the Middle Georgia region for over 90 years.

Newby's Ranks Among

CORDELE, GA., DISPATCH, Friday, February 28, 1975 Page 10

Dooly's Oldest Businesses

By ROBERT NEWBY

Back in the early days of 1890 when Richwood, Georgia was the terminal point for the old Georgia Southern and Florida Railroad, Newbys opened their first retail store in Dooly County. This Dooly County outlet was an experimental barometer of Robert Ruskin Newby of Wilkerson County whose grandson, William Franklin Newby, managed.

When the G.S.&F. Railroad work gang moved on southward and the old Parrott Lumber Company shut down their operations, W.F. Newby moved to Vienna. The store was first located on the spur track of the G.S.&F just above what is now known as Thompson Supply Company. It was a shotgun type wooden building and the store was a general merchandise establishment. The next move was to the South side of Union Street in the vicinity of the location of Nutt's Barbership in Vienna.

In the spring of 1908 when plans for the old American Banking Corporation building were being drawn up and the block of buildings adjoining was under construction, W.F. Newby moved into the present location now occupied by the store.

Many old heirloom objects gathered by the retail establishment have been lost over the years. One of the oldest, cash registers and probably one of the earliest made store-type wall clocks were lost from Newbys old store back in 1967 when the complete stock was sold to make room for another expansion and new merchandise that was shipped in for the expansion of that year. The company that bought the stock

allowed the movers to take many items of historical interest that were not included in the sale and they were never recovered.

The oldest peanut roaster, one that was wound up like a clock and was heated with kerosene oil, has been lost and it is suspected that it disappeared when a storm of several years back destroyed the old Newby barn where many other antiques were stored.

This peanut parcher was the first vehicle to launch Robert L. Newby, Jr. into the business venture of Newbys back in 1923 when his grandfather put him to work as a lad of 4½ years. Up and through the years of 1960 this machine and several others more modern and eventually with electric power were the beginning for many young men in this area with their first experience with commerce. Selling peanuts was the first job young men had at Newbys and they were later moved into the store as clerks as they grew older.

One of the services that Newbys innovated in Vienna under the management of W.F. Newby was a house-to-house delivery. Jack Gammage, a long deceased Negro helper drove the horse and dray wagon as it made its regular morning deliveries that usually were telephoned into the store during the early morning hours, which by the way, were from 6 a.m. weekdays and 5 a.m. Saturdays until 2 a.m. Sunday morning.

Back in those days Dooly County had a population of over 18,000 people and most of them were farmers. By the time they drove to town with their two horse wagons and shopped, it was after midnight, for many before they begin their homeward

trek....And driving in a two horse wagon 10 to 20 miles was no easy task. The customers for the most part were carried on credit accounts from one fall to the next and there was no thought given about the honesty of those who traded.

Depressions and disasters have been regular occurrances in our trade territory but we have never had one that the Lord wasn't sufficient helping men and their families to overcome. Dooly County has never been a county to experience very great times of affluence, but it has been a place that folks have always had enough to fill their needs. This comes about because we are a Christian Community.

The Newby family have been in their stewardship for many centures, coming first to England with William the Conqueror in the year 1066, from their native land of France where they were general merchants and bankers. Out of respect for Robert the 1st, Duke of Normandy, who also was the father of William the

Conqueror or family has continously used the surname of Robert and William throughout all these many years.

The French name for our family was 'De Nubie and it was later anglicized in the year 1231 as Newby. The Newby family became Englishmen due to their loyalty and aid given to William the Conqueror on his invasion in 1066. After the war William gave all of his supporters large tracts of land and titles.

There is a large palace in Northern England near Ripon that is named Newby Hall. The original grant was for 40,000 acres. Today this has been reduced to 8,000 acres, but it is

Fig. 120 Newby's Store

Robert L. Newby III

Melody Newby,

Robert L. Newby, Jr.

Marie Newby,

Robert L. Newby

Melissa Newby

IX. Related Families

John Mohr McIntosh, Chief of the Barclum Branch of the Clan McIntosh in Scotland, came to America as one of a colony of Highlanders, and was one of the founders of the town of Inverness (Iater to be called Darien) at the mouth of the Altamaha River in Georgia. Sailing from Scotland in October 1735, he arrived in Georgia in January 1736. Of the colony at New Inverness he was Civil Commandant, later being ordered by General Oglethorpe to raise a company of Highlanders. for service against the Spanish at St. Augustine, Florida. He was captured at St. Augustine and carried a prisoner to Spain where he languished for a long time. Shortlyafter his return to Georgia he died. **John Mohr McIntosh** was born in Bedeneck, Scotland, 24th March 1700. He was the son of Lachlan McIntosh of Knocknagil, by his wife, Mary, daughter of John Lockhart, the. Baillie of Inverness.

Robert Baillie married **Ann McIntosh, only** daughter of **John Mohr McIntosh.** Their children were, John, whose oldest son Robert inherited Coulter house on the death of his Uncle James and returned to Scotland, Gilleland, James, Mazey, Catherine, Ann who married her Cousin Lac Ian McIntosh, the son of Col. William, **Mary Ann, who married Judge Wm. Davies. Robert** Baille was a Lieutenant in the British Militia, a Tory during the Revolutionary War. However it is said that there continued to be a warm relationship between his Mc Intosh in –laws and himself during and after the War. This is quite remarkable to me given the McIntosh activities during the War and the hot animosity of the two combatant forces.

Edward Davies, Member of the Rebel Assembly of Georgia. (see Jones History of Georgia Vol 2, F 422), was named by Colonial Gov. Jas. Wright as a traitor to the Crown(page 452). **Edward** married **Rebecca Lloyd** the daughter of Benj. L1QYd, all of Savannah. They had only one son **Judge William Davies.** Edward Davies was co-director Ins. office Sept.16, "777-1779. They had one child, **William Davies.**

William Davies became a lawyer of distinction. When not on the bench, he was a partner of John McPherson Berrian. In 1816 he was appointed Judge of the U. S. District Court for the District of Georgia and served with distinction. In 1828 he was appointed Judge of the Superior Courts of the Circuit, embracing Chatham and the contiguous counties in Georgia. He was never robust physically and it is though that the intense application of the duties of his office broke his health and he died rather suddenly in April 1829 and is buried in the old cemetery in Savannah, Georgia. (Colonial Cemetery Savannah)

William Davies married **Mary Ann Baillie,** daughter of **Robert Baillie and Ann McIntosh.** Their children were John Bulloch, Ann, **Robert Baillie,** Mary and Euphemia. He was born in Savannah Jan 8, 1776.He was a Cornett, Vol. Tr. Light Dragoons, 4th Squad, 2nd Lt. Vol Co. Art., 1 st Regt.

Chatham Co., Ga. Militia (Savannah) Dec. 15, 1812. **William Davies** married **Mary Ann Baillie,** daughter of **Robert Baillie and Ann McIntosh.** Their children were John Bulloch, Ann, **Robert Baillie (Berrien),** Mary Euphenia.

Robert Berrien lBaille) Davies Member

House of Rep., Dooly County, 1842

Member of Senate, Dooly County 1843

Clerk of Superiorand Inferior Courts, Dooly County, Jan 22, 1848–1864.

He married **Miss Louise Jane** Key of Dooly County, Georgia. At the time of his death in 1864 he was clerk of the Superior Court of Dooly County. His children were William, Alfred, Robert, Mary Anne - Taylor, Charles, Walter **Paulette,** and Sarah Franklin Stebbins.

X. Vienna memories 1945-1960

Fig. 121 Gert & Jack ca. 1975

I do not think one can describe all the joys of Vienna visits for our family. We were loved by so many people and were showered with gifts and meals. Family for us was everywhere. Joe let me work at the soda fountain in the summer. I was not very good and did not project a happy attitude, but I was happy to be there and did learn the trade. We sold "Welfare Specials" for 7 cents for a large cup with ice. It was the size of a large fountain Coke, a 10 cent charge, but was made by holding the lever down to fill the cup. That gave one serving of Coke syrup and the rest was soda water and ice. With a lemon or lime slice it was a bargain!

Jim, Johnny Pharr and I worked some at Newby's Store at the cigarette, cigar, and candy counter. We also operated the peanut machine which stood just outside the store front door. We did a good business and worked the cash register which was big time business at our age. We tallied up at the end of the day and got some responsibility along with our salary.

The Vienna Theater was a popular place on Saturday afternoons and we went with cousins and friends like Lawrence and Billy Lowe Nutt. We were most interested in Cowboy movies and serials like Whip Wilson and Lash LaRue. As we got older Aunt Al Forbes would take us to Cordele and a larger movie theater. She also took us to Roobins Department store in Cordele and bought us clothes from time to time. She was the most generous person to all her nephews and nieces I have ever known. She and Joe had no children but she enjoyed all the children and saw that they had everything to keep them happy on their visits.

My summers in Vienna and the Christmas vacations obviously hold fond memories. I have some more of those in the next Appendix but they vary from the mainline family history. So seek them if you wish.

XI. Further notes on Vienna Georgia experiences

Kaiser-Frazier automobiles looked more like the "Batmobile" than any production car I ever saw. I remember a dealership located about one block off the southern end of the square in Vienna, the county seat of Dooly County Georgia. There was another one in downtown Athens Ga although the one in Vienna was probably one of the smallest in existence. It was owned by my friend Jadyboy Peavey's father. His dad was named J. D. Peavey so they called his son Jadyboy. It may have been spelled Jadieboy but I never saw it written, just spoken. I thought it typical of southern nomenclature that such a name would be accepted. That line of automobiles did not last very long and was never popular. I suspect a run of five years may have been the lifespan of K-F. They seemed to me to be a trial venture immediately after the end of WWII, so this would be about 1948 to 1951. (A recent Google search proved that Henry J. Kaiser and Joe Frazier built their cars on the theory that post war times would be good for cars. They apparently disagreed on philosophy and parted ways in 1953. The pictures I now see show some "Batmobile" trend in 1947 but much more in 1953.)

My immediate family lived in Athens Georgia at that time. We always lived within a fifty mile radius of Atlanta, in Athens, Marietta, or Gainesville. Atlanta was the Hub of our state. My Big Mamma and Big Daddy lived in Atlanta so I had some intimate contact with the city. It was my home from 1956 to 1960 when I attended Emory University in Decatur. Emory at that time was touted, by those who I knew, to be a site of educational excellence and proclaimed itself to be the "Harvard of the South"-although I doubt that Harvard or Duke gave that subtitle much credence. Vienna was far to the south of Atlanta but still considered "Middle Georgia" and the natives denied a designation of "South Georgia"- a provincial distinction of local significance.

While a North Georgian by birth and paternal lineage, my maternal roots were distinctly Middle Georgian. I was tied to Dooly County through Christmas and Summer Vacations for the first two decades of my life and spiritually for my entire lifetime. The little known verse of the Classic song Georgia on My Mind points out that "Melodies, like Memories, are Treasures of the Heart" and surely those days visiting relatives and Dooly county friends created many "treasures" that lasted forever. I know the memories are embellished and partially remembered, but they are a pleasant retreat. They include recall of sunshine, heavy, warm, rainfall, trips to the swimming pool, treasures found at the Vienna 5 and 10 cent store, comic books from Kitchen's Drugstore, and Saturday westerns at the Vienna Theater -The Last Picture Show of Middle Georgia not Texas location.

Jadyboy was my friend and we spent many hot days in his backyard climbing pecan trees and learning it was easier to go up than down without a shocking drop. He lived up Union Street from my Grandmother Burr's house. The name Union was an unlikely place name for a staunchly Confederate locale, but since my Big Mamma lived on Confederate Avenue in Atlanta, one block downhill from Grant Park we assumed peace was at hand.

Booth Tarkington or Mark Twain would have trouble imagining names or personalities more colorful than my friends of those days. The troubles of today, drugs, crime, or childhood abductions, were not known in those days of 1944 to 1953. We had not yet reached the threats encountered by James Dean in "Rebel Without a Cause" or the more fearful" Blackboard Jungle" with its gang activity. Instead we climbed chinaberry trees, made homemade slingshots with berries for ammunition, and actually shot each other with peas in a peashooter. We walked everywhere- to the movies on Saturdays and to the Union Street pool until it closed. I was not happy when Vienna built a public pool further away from town. I swam in both but the Union Street Pool was my favorite. Jadyboy, Lawrence Nutt, and Billy Lowe Nutt and I spent entire days at the pool with only a break for lunch. One summer I developed an ear infection after a full day at the pool. I was treated that warm afternoon with Sweet oil and bed rest. When the chimes struck at the Methodist Church, I thought I had come to my end with ear pain. Somehow I survived and returned to the pool yet again. In later years I was told that in South Georgia one could get a fungus in the ear from swimming pools and if you dripped alcohol into the ear canal after each swim the infection would not develop. Maybe that could be applied in Middle Georgia as well. I used that alcohol technique years later in Augusta, Georgia at the Phi Chi pool as there was no shortage of alcohol.

I don't think we knew much about girls at that age of 10-13. I did notice the model airplanes that a visiting boyfriend made and gave to my cousin Mary Tharpe. Solid model making was a personal hobby at the time. These boyfriend-made models were so special that I could only view them through the glass case where they resided-no touching. Mary and Shirley were my older cousins and not interested my activities. Jadyboy had a sister named Mary Laura, a friend of my cousins but we stayed away from these "older girls".

Billy Lowe and Lawrence Nutt lived toward the railroad track on Union Street and only two doors from Burr's house. They were both my "very, very, best, good friends". Mr. Nutt, their father, was the town barber and he cut my hair in the summer seasonal buzz cut on many occasions. His shop adjoined my Uncle Joe Forbes's Drug Store in town. I spent many days in the "Nutt house" sharing meals and lessons on life. The Nutts adhered to the rules of the Christian faith and their home was a pleasure to visit. Billy Lowe was the wisest, strongest, and most knowledgeable of my friends. He was two or three years older than Lawrence and me. He knew about things important to boys. He created the Black Panther Club for me and Lawrence and identified a special password and grip .He played basketball for Vienna High and knew the legends of the Vienna "Wonder Five" who had won the state championship years before and were never forgotten. He knew the attributes of Lash Larue over Whip Wilson and who Tom Mix was. I only knew common things like "Champion was Gene Autry's horse" and that "Roy Rogers was married to Dale Evans", who my Big Mamma thought we may be some kin with-her being an Evans by birth.

Fig. 122 Out Where a Friend is a Friend

Billy knew things like Audrey Murphy's being the most decorated soldier in WWII and that while being short, he was brave and courageous. Lawrence and I never crossed Billy Lowe and he never let us down by doing any wrong or teasing us. He always was on the right side of any discussion and followed the rules mandated by grown-ups. Later when I went to Viet Nam and arrived with my company in Danang, we went into "hooch" to cool down and drink cokes. I got a shock of my life. Someone found that we had mail which had traveled faster than we did on the month long boat ride. One of on the letters was from my mother telling me that Billie Lowe Nutt had died while training to "auto-rotate" a helicopter landing at Fort Rucker Alabama. Even at the end of his life Billy was trying to do the right thing and had volunteered to fly helicopters in Vietnam. I had at that time just completed the Counter Insurgency School at the John F .Kennedy U. S. Special Forces School at Fort Bragg. I had finished one year internship after medical school and considered myself to be advanced in life experiences. Nevertheless I could not withhold tears at losing an old and very special friend who had played a significant role in my early years. I know the loss and later adjustment was difficult for Lawrence and his family. A boy named Ed lived in a large house on Church Street behind Burr's house on Union and just up the street from my Aunt Sity's house. He taught me about stick model airplanes covered with tissue paper and powered by rubber band motors. These required more attention to detail than the solid balsa models in which I specialized. It was a horror to me to see Ed light a match to airplane glue on the tail of a plane and send it into the air. What a loss after all the time and patience! But I must say it was quite a sight to see. And there was always the joy of making another plane, bigger and more powerful. Skeeter White, who had white hair, was another summer friend in Vienna around the pool. With a summer haircut, he seemed to be almost without hair. His eyes attracted the Dooly County gnats in an excessive fashion. On occasion they gathered around the eye sockets to make mobile mascara of a rather startling configuration. He was adept in "blowing" them away but they seemed to immediately return on the hottest and most humid days. Billy Lowe had taught me to "blow gnats" so I had developed that middle Georgia skill myself, even though I was from North Georgia where gnats were not prominent. I used that demonstration later in front of the South Georgia boys I met at Emory, giving me some brotherhood with that foreign element. Blowing gnats is still a worthy skill but is negated somewhat when wearing glasses.

The Nutts and I went to the Methodist Campground if I was in Vienna on the proper date. They never missed that event and were loyal members of the Vienna Methodist Church long before it was renamed the Vienna United Methodist Church. The Campground week was a multifunctional occasion. Spiritual enrichment was the primary purpose and the Preaching and Singing was wonderful. A large Tabernacle was the center and most impressive structure of the Grounds. This was rebuilt during my memory and my dad drew a rendering of the new structure which many people still possess. The floor was covered with fresh straw and benches were available and equipped with cardboard fans stapled to flat sticks. The local funeral homes were advertised on the fan itself so they must have been donated to the Meeting. These were not ornamental and were used continuously during the services both for gnats and stifling heat. The visiting preachers were motivating with their sermons and were well received, especially by the adult ladies of the church who apparently appreciated the variety of the messages.

A secondary purpose of the Camp Meeting, but not one of lesser importance to the youth, was the socialization. Perhaps Camp Meeting served as a lessening of tension in the initial fraternization between adolescent males and females. To me, somewhat of an outsider, the friendly nature of the females was unique, flattering, and attractive. Between the older teens I feel sure it included physical interaction. Thirdly this occasion provided a family gathering, a return to a rustic style of living, and endless food and desserts. My Aunt AL had two "cabins" at the campground. These provided sleeping space in beds and on pallets spread on the floors. Since the "Grounds" were only two miles from Vienna, Robert Junior and Joe Forbes who worked in town came and went frequently. My dad was on vacation as well as Uncle Kelly Pharr, so they participated in the whole Camp. Dad was friendly with the preachers and local men and was quite popular with the group despite his Baptist leanings. A creek ran behind the cabin and the other cousins and I splashed and fished daily. There was a dam across the creek closed to the main grounds and from time to time a lake formed enough for swimming. My mother, Gertrude, told me stories of her times at Camp Meeting and her history made this a time worn treat.Not far from the entry to the Campgrounds and down a dirt road, often cross striped with washboard ruts, was my Cousin Robert Newby's farm. He had a man living on the farm named Rooster and we marked our bearings by Rooster's house. Jay was a hired man, who my dad said could plow the straightest row for planting that could be measured, did most of the work on the farm planting peanuts, cotton, and peaches. Robert Junior operated a Peach business from road side stands and shipping to the Farmer's Market in Atlanta. He had business cards printed showing a Cat's head and announcing "Good Pussy Peaches". He would pass out the cards with a great laugh for which he was famous. This was a "side business" for him as he ran Newby's Store as well as a Dodge dealership. He ran for the legislature and was on the Board of the Bank of Vienna for many years. He named himself the "Duke of Dooly" after a trip to England and a superficial genealogy study. He truly was the most outstanding personality in our family. When he visited Bristol the first time he had me take him to the Pointer Overall Manufacturing plant because he had sold those overalls in his store for years, as had his dad Robert and my grandfather, W.F. Newby. When he met Mr. King who operated the factory for his family, Robert told him that in Dooly his family had fought the King and were part of the new Republic, not receiving Grants from the King. It should have been obvious that the Kings also were Revolutionaries as they had settled on recent Indian lands, not on land grants. Robert drove several Corvettes through the years and said he wanted to be buried sitting upright in his Corvette, but it did not turn out to happen that way. During WWII Robert flew PBYs in the Pacific and cut quite a wide path in his white dress Navy uniform driving his convertible down Union Street with his young wife Marie by his side. That sight was the envy of many a young men in the county. When Robert owned the farm we were hosted to Dove shoots one or two times a year. Cousin Newby Kelt, another Naval aviator in the Korean conflict, organized the NCODDS. This was Navy jargon for Newby Clan Opening Day Dove Shoots. For years we did not miss an opening day regardless of the heat.

It was near September 1 yearly and Dooly was still in the summer season. Sitting in a field with hunting jacket filled with shells was a challenge. Newby named my Dad "Tail Gunner" or "Long Shot" for his ability to bring down the birds too high for everyone else. We ate dove for breakfast and dinner after some of those shoots. The family used these occasions to gather and visit.

Often we would go to the "River" in Cordele the evening after the hunt. Daphne's was a desired fish camp where we consumed large quantities of fried fish, hush puppies, and ice tea. There was also bourbon available for the adults, in significant quantities on some instances. The family was always joking and fun to be around. My Mother especially became known for telling stories at the prodding of relatives. With time she perfected this performance and I think enjoyed the opportunity. She took this talent back to her friends at home and became moderately famous for her talent. She had one story which was the favorite of the crowd that she always told about Archiball Assholebrook. The next in popularity was about a man who ordered a tailor made suit but on the final fitting found that it was terribly asymmetrical with one leg and one arm too short. The clever tailor coached the purchaser in retracting one leg and one arm so the hems seemed long enough. When he went out on the street one lady commented how deformed that poor man was, and her friend said "yes but don't his suit fit good!" She had one short story about the lady of the house having a baby at the time her hired cook had hers. At age 1 the family marveled at the mistress' baby saying "bye –bye". With that said after much coaching, the cook's baby in a crib in the kitchen sat up and said,"Where ya'll going?"

XII. Newby Kelt comments on a Georgia Game Trip from Vienna

Gene Methvin(Vienna native who became the Editor of the Reader's Digest) sent a note that reminded me of a distant time in 1949 when Georgia played Furman in football on one of the coldest days known to the then living human beings in the State of Georgia.

While waiting for my assigned slot in Navy Flight Training in Pensacola, I was temporarily filling in at Vienna High School for a teacher who had been drafted. [Korean War and all that]. Eleventh and twelfth grade Health, Algebra, Trigonometry, and Geometry. After class hours I coached Boy's as well as Girl's basketball. As you might imagine, this schedule pretty much filled my day.

I also drove the basketball teams to away games in an ancient Bluebird School Bus. For which, of course, I had no large vehicle license nor any experience driving a bus. Most team members were delivered to the school grounds for departure, but returning late at night presented other problems, leading me to learn many of the by-ways and dirt roads of Dooly County.

As fall turned into winter, the School received a gracious note from the University of Georgia inviting the senior students to attend the Georgia/Furman football game. One can easily deduce that tickets to this game were not selling well and there might be some potential enrollees in a group of Vienna H.S. Seniors vastly impressed by the UGA campus and its football team cheerfully administering cruel punishment to a hapless foe. The school accepted the invitation and we soon had the tickets. The Seniors were ecstatic.

The day before the long awaited trip the radio warned of a severe cold front, along with the usual reports of hog and cattle prices on the Mercantile Exchanges. Having lived some years in Athens while at the University I had some bitter cold weather memories. The students had none. Cold is not the same when one can dash out and in of a house instead of sitting for hours on a concrete bench in a stadium. But youth and enthusiasm conquered age and common sense and in the early morning we departed for Athens. Gaily singing songs of Victory to come.

I soon discovered that the rubber gasket meant to plug the hole containing the accelerator pedal was missing. I had not noticed this during the warm days of fall, and even if I had I doubt the School budget would have included that minor repair. In any event the temperature was in the low teens and the bus had no heater. I pulled into a rest stop to allow visits to the facilities. I tried to plug the pedal hole with paper towels as the fifty mile an hour breeze up my right pant leg was really punishing. As time passed the paper seemed to melt away. I pulled over again and took the sock from my left foot, put the shoe back on, and stuffed my sock into the gap. It was good enough to prevent frostbite and we got to Athens and went directly to the Stadium.

Folks, let me truly tell you it was very, very cold.

We had a female chaperone with us, whose name escapes me at this late date, and we conferred on how much more of this the Seniors, or we, could take. We had made it to half-time and our collective decision was that that would have to suffice and we must head for Vienna.

The youngsters looked quite pitifully cold, but some still maintained that we should not give up so easily. Perhaps these were the descendents of those who gave the Yankees more than they wanted.

I drove us to the SAE House [my old Fraternity] and asked Doc Banks, the legendary "Major Domo" of the House to make a large batch of hot chocolate to thaw my passengers a little. Doc also gave me some old rags and a piece of string to plug the pedal hole.

In a way the trip home was anticlimactic. The gas pedal hole plug held up; the Seniors slept the deep sleep of teenage exhaustion and I repeatedly told myself to be more careful about selecting the things I agreed to do. The fact that I spent the next twenty years flying on and off Carrier decks proves that lecturing yourself may not always be a success.

But the Vienna High School trip to the Georgia/Furman Game was a success and I would wager that all those who were on that journey remember it vividly to this very day.

Love to you and yours, Newby Kelt

XIII. Nan Campbell Eaton Recollections of Family

Nan is my first Cousin and the Daughter of Billie Evelyn Butterworth Campbell and Milton Orson Campbell. This is her story of her family and Grandmother George Wilberth Evans Butterworth. It is tellingly descriptive and needs no editorializing by me.

I can't tell the history of my family without telling the history of our home, Georgia, and the faith in God that my family has had as far back as we have records. My ancestors; Campbell and Butterworth, Evans and Pope, Benton, Wilson, Hughes and Knox – all of these families were settlers in Georgia, most settling early enough to fight for independence in the Revolutionary War. My family contributed to the establishment of this country, this state and many different communities. They were doctors, judges, statesmen, educators, bankers, and soldiers – and their strong, loving, creative, talented and resourceful women who bore them, married them or came from them kept their lives, their legacy, their traditions and their heritage alive through these stories. Being the youngest of my generation in the Butterworth clan I don't remember these events or some of these people. But I do remember being able to sit and listen to my family members tell of these things. I was truly blessed to have this time with Big Mama when she was older and had the time to sit and reminisce. There were many opportunities to sit in her living room and listen to her talk with mama, Sue and Mary. So many times events were remembered and facets of the same event revealed by other participants until the event seemed very real and quite vivid. But this is about Big Mama and I want to send to you, with love, some of my favorite memories – in stories.

I think this whole story actually begins in Canton, Georgia with George Washington Evans. There is history of those that came before him, but not personal history – this was Big Mama's daddy. He was raised through hard work and talent in that crossroad of a town nestled at the end of the Appalachian Mountains. When his brothers went off to fight in the War Between the States, he was made to stay home because he was too young and was needed to help work the farm. But as the War lingered on, GW was most useful in loading up supplies and fresh horses from home and taking them to his brothers and the men from his community fighting this war. Then, one day he loaded up what supplies they could scrape together at home, rode off and joined his brothers in the Confederate Army. He never talked a lot about it but his company fought throughout Tennessee and he was there in the fight to defend Georgia from Sherman and that command as they took a broad swath through his homeland stealing, burning and destroying everything of worth.

When his brother was wounded in battle, GW left to take him home so that he could be nursed back to health, but his brother died en route. GW did not stay for the funeral but went back to join his company in the fight.

Soon enough our army lost and we became an occupied nation with bitter Yankee soldiers and carpetbaggers taking control and delivering contempt for any man that fought for the Confederacy. An exceptionally hard time.

But he was a young man, aged by his experience, but determined to rise and prosper through his knowledge of horses. Through breeding and trading he purchased wagons for delivery and bred mules for farming and soon opened a livery stable.

Then, in 1870 he married Buena Knox who came from a genteel family and the young couple started their family of seven children. He was a very able and shrewd businessman – and the mule trade was prosperous – so soon he became one of Canton Georgia's best established business owners.

It was in 1890 when the seventh and final child in the family with two brothers and four sisters was born. Maybe it was because her parents knew there would be no more children and named the baby girl George after her daddy that as a child she was quite the tomboy. Her mother pressed her older sisters into the knowledge of etiquette and decorum, and they were very feminine and quite lovely, but George was not interested in girl stuff. She enjoyed going to the stables and exercising the horses and the job was every day all year long.

By the time she was twelve she was quite a horseman and the sight of the young girl with copper hair galloping all out down dirt roads around Canton no longer caused any commotion. Except for the one and only time she was caught standing in the saddle picking apples and stuffing them in her shirt to take back to the stables for the horses, she was an honest and happy child and stayed out of trouble and out of the way.

It was a busy time in the family as the children grew, married and had children of their own. It was a new century and everything was changing – life was exciting.

Then in the year that the Wright brothers successfully took flight and George was thirteen, her beloved mother, Buena Vista Wilbreth Knox Evans died. George was devastated. She was also just a young turn-of-the-century teenager living at home with her sixteen year old brother and her father. But she was turning into a young lady and her mother and sisters were all gone – just when she needed them most.

What she didn't know was that she had been noticed riding those roads with that red hair pulled back in a braid like an Indian.

Virgil Butterworth was a couple of calendar years older but ages more mature. His dad had died of pneumonia from ferrying people to safety during a flood of the Etowah River when Virgil was just ten years old. He left school and went to work to support his mother, three sisters and one younger brother when he was just fourteen.

So, when he and George were married the Sunday before Christmas, 1907, they moved in with his mother and family. Virgil's mother, Sarilda Ann Hughes Butterworth, took young George under her wing and taught her everything she knew, and since George knew nothing, that took a while! Although she had been well taken care of, with housekeepers, maids and cooks, she now had to learn to do many of the skills and duties that had been assigned to servants - but she remembers those days as some of her best memories. Mrs. Butterworth had been raised in the traditional Scot/Irish traditions and was gentle and patient in teaching all of her daughters the art of "home management". She was quite talented in her handwork- most especially sewing. She taught her daughters (and Big Mama) how to sew so well that one of her daughters was employed by one of Atlanta's 'finest' ladies as a seamstress. This lady traveled the world and would come back to Atlanta from Paris or New York and ask Milam to alter her new clothes. Milam would take the garments apart to see how they were constructed, alter them, then construct a pattern and duplicate the piece for her employer- and at a fraction of the price she had paid for the original. But as Milam was developing her skills, at the same time she was teaching all of the sisters at home how to do the same work. Big Mama shared with her Evans sisters as well, so all of the women in both our families were always equipped with a well constructed and very fashionable wardrobe.

Big Mama had the best of all worlds, as she was a confident, well established woman who also had the talent and skill of doing most anything she wanted and the blessing of a very adoring, godly husband.

Virgil had worked his way up to where he was making a good living in the marble business. Not only was he strong but he was also very artistic, and he had been promoted to supervisory positions because of his ability to earn the respect and cooperation of his fellow workers. (Jack, you can tell a lot more about Big Daddy)

Then in 1918, GW had had enough. Maybe it was time to move on. But this would be a huge move; after all he was now seventy-one years old! And he really was in a pretty good position in Canton. But he had lost his wife, a son-in-law had died, and then a couple of years later his daughter also died leaving their three children orphaned and the responsibility of their divorced aunt. World War I had ended and Canton had grown into a large community, the livery had turned into a thriving delivery service – but at his age, the joy of work was over. He wanted to make things better for his family.

So he had decided. He took the train south one morning and came back home that night to let his family know that they were all – every one of them – moving to Atlanta.

(Brenda will fill in about where they moved in Atlanta)

George and Virgil with their children Jack, Sue and Mary moved with him. And a year after the family moved, the best part of the story happened... at least for me. Because that year, Congress approved the 19th amendment to the Constitution giving women the right to vote; Theodore Roosevelt died; the Volstead Act passed beginning prohibition in the United States; and... GW Evans' last grandchild was born in Atlanta. It was a beautiful red haired baby girl named Billie.

At some point, Virgil got a job at Berkeley granite on Confederate Avenue and he moved his family into a lovely house close by. On one occasion, soon after the move, GW came by to visit George and the children. While he was there, a salesman came by to take measurements and discuss the purchase of awnings with George. He climbed the stairs to the house and waiting on the porch with his fabric samples. Big Mama greeted him and was carefully turning through the samples as her father sat on the porch and listened. The salesman was assured of the sale and anxious for his customer to make her selection and complete the order, so he thought he would just help her make up her mind.

This ended as a most unfortunate decision, for as soon as he "highly recommended the lovely FEDERAL blue as it goes so well with the PLAIN GREY house"... he had to gather his samples and run down the stairs as Big Mama actually held her elderly Confederate veteran father as he threatened to beat him with his walking cane.

There was a Veterans' Home down the street from Big Mama and I don't remember anyone telling of GW going to visit but mama mentioned the kids going past and talking to the Confederate veterans often. It was on Confederate Avenue and around the corner from where Big Daddy worked.

Big Mama and Big Daddy were very fortunate to have a good job and a nice house. They were both aware of their blessings and shared generously with family and clergy and as they could with friends and neighbors. On one occasion they had asked the preacher to join them for Sunday dinner and Big Mama had splurged on the biggest chicken she could buy. Before they all filed out of the house to go to church, Big Mama told each family member that there would only be one piece of chicken each. Now the way Big Mama cut up the bird, there would be nine pieces of chicken. For dinner there would be the preacher, Big Daddy, Big Mama, Jack, Sue, Mary and little Billie, leaving the extra pieces for Big Daddy and the preacher.

So with all preparations in place and the family's cooperation, after church the dinner was served. Everyone laughed at little Billie, for as she was placed in her high chair she was already reaching for the chicken. The prayer was said and when everyone opened their eyes, Billie had her piece of chicken, happily eating away. As the dinner progressed, Billie started asking for "chick-chick", but Big Mama had moved the chicken platter to the other side of the table. The conversation continued with a small voice singing in the background "chick-chick-chick????" But the small voice got louder, and louder, until Jack quickly finished his meal and took little Billie for a walk, her clucking all the way out the door.

As the family grew, Big Mama continued to cook three large meals a day. She would get up very early and by the time Big Daddy and Jack were dressed for work there would be ham, sausage, bacon, grits, gravy, home-made biscuits, coffee and home-made jam hot and ready.

Soon after breakfast, Sally would arrive. Sally was a large black Atlanta born woman who was the only paid member of the family. She would ride the bus then walk up the stairs and into the house. She would put away her coat, pocketbook and gloves then tie on an apron and a headscarf twisted and tucked until all of her hair was covered. She would then "take over" the kitchen.

At dinner time, Big Daddy would return home with Jack and very often other men with whom he worked. There would be fresh vegetables, casseroles, stews, soups, salads and desserts of every make and kind. Big Mama and Sally were both exceptional cooks, but Big Mama was THE master of creating full meals out of any provisions she happened to have on hand at the time. A skill that was primary in keeping her family healthy and unafraid even during the peak of the depression.

It was a very hard time, but opportunities arose for some family fun, too. One year, Big Daddy had some sort of business in Charleston, South Carolina, so he loaded up his family and Sally and they rented a house on the beach for a week.

The entertainment was being with each other – swimming or walking the beach – jigsaw puzzles – card games – and just relaxing in the summer breeze. That is for everyone except Sally.

She had packed what she needed to be able to cook for that huge crowd for a whole week, but she still needed to buy some things to supplement what she had brought to cook. So, every morning a local man would drive by the vacation cottages to sell vegetables and fish to the visitors. Every morning Sally would listen for his cart then tear out of the house to see what he had and get what they needed before anyone else could pick over his offerings or even worse, get the good stuff.

Sally must have been attractive because the salesman would spend quite a lot of time talking to her and flirting with her because she took a lot of kidding from the family. But they were most impressed with the quality of the meals she presented that week.

One night, when the family had finished the most delicious fish dinner they had ever experienced, they asked Sally what kind of fish her "friend" had delivered for the feast.

Without even looking up she replied, "I shor' am glad you enjoyed it but there Ain't no way I can tell you what it was. That Geechee man – he don't talk right! I don't understan' a word he say!"

I still think that it is extraordinary that Big Daddy could take his family on trips like this when times were so very hard. But he and Big Mama managed very well. Mama mentioned often that Big Daddy would come home from work and the room would be full of children and cousins sitting or playing everywhere, and Big Daddy would look around the room then ask "where is everybody?" when the only person in the house not in that room would be Big Mama. He never tried to hide how much he loved his bride.

I don't remember my grandfather Butterworth, or Big Daddy, except for his pushing me in the swing when I was very young. (That swing is in my backyard in Mansfield) But I do remember how much he was loved and dearly missed by all after he died. During the depression, Big Daddy "helped" many of his friends from North Georgia by finding jobs for the men and keeping many struggling families afloat. My Big Daddy and Uncle Jack designed and delivered hundreds of the stone memorials in cemeteries in Atlanta and West View was primarily outfitted by Berkley Marble (ironically, that is where Big Daddy and Big Mama are buried, but they only have a bronze headstone). I have a little soapstone lamb that Big Daddy carved and gave to mama after he had used it as a model for some work he did. Big Daddy was a very tall man and by all accounts, humorous, caring and very gentle. He had many, many friends who were devoted. He was a Mason and a charter member of Confederate Avenue Baptist Church. He was generous to a fault and devoted to his entire family. He and Big Mama helped to raise all of his brothers and sisters, then their own four children, and then their brother's and sister's children after several untimely deaths.

There are lots of remembrances of the time before and when Big Daddy died, but they were very heart wrenching. He was very, VERY loved and deeply missed.

But the family grew and the family lost those whom they loved. And time moved on.

When I was a pre-teen – too young to go to camp and too old to be underfoot all summer – mama sent me to Atlanta to spend a whole week with my grandmothers.

When I went to see Big Mama, her house smelled of the most delicious dishes – and cookies – and bath powder – and a hint of Pine Sol. We always went to church, even on week days! She had a one story house on a hill with a thousand wide slate steps going up from Confederate Avenue to heaven. On the top of that hill she had a porch that led into a sweet cottage with beautiful furniture and carefully selected pictures, handwork and very interesting 'stuff'. She had a little kitchen with a pantry but her refrigerator was on her "side" porch that started at the kitchen and wrapped around to the back of the house, going down stairs to the "sitting" porch. The "sitting" porch was my favorite because the floor was made of all different granite and marble slabs patched together in cement and when the sun filtered through the magnolia in the back yard the stone just sparkled.

During my stay with Big Mama we worked on craft things; like sticking toothpick-and-crêpe paper parasols into place cards for a dinner for visiting missionaries from Japan. We played Scrabble and all sorts of board games; or she would read her Bible while I played with little plastic boxes filled with tiny samples of lipstick; or we polished our nails with one of the many bottles of RED polish lined up carefully in a woven basket.

At night I would have to climb a set of stairs (that Uncle Fred made) to ascend to the tallest bed I have ever seen, covered in beautiful handwork and smelling fresh-off-the-clothesline. I would lie there and listen to the lions roar all night at the Grant's Park Zoo on Boulevard up the hill.

We always dressed up every day and she even took me downtown to Rich's Magnolia Room for lunch. I do remember riding the bus and after getting on while Big Mama paid the driver, trying to go sit at the back of the bus but being "shooed" away by the black women when I tried to go past.

It seemed that Big Mama knew everybody in Atlanta – and Atlanta was a BIG town! I never saw her without earrings, a necklace made of some sort of beads, a dress (heavens NO she NEVER wore pants!!!) and that red nail polish. She wore a hat when she went to church on Sundays but we got away with not wearing it during the week.

She would cook the most wonderful meals but she was notorious for two things: praying long and intricate prayers while you would sit and smell and ache to begin eating but had to wait and hear about Jackie in Viet Nam, Jim in college, every other grandchild and what they were doing, every other cousin, then when the family was completed she started on every missionary in the Southern Baptist Church to the point that she even opened a book during her prayer and read off names and a list of their needs that they had printed out and distributed. You could just watch the food get cold; then when Big Mama was finished with her meal and was ready to clear the table – she did, whether you were finished or not!

I will never forget Big Mama after Faye died. She was living alone, probably the first time in her life, and the beautiful neighborhood on Confederate Avenue had gone to trash and scary people. Big Mama no longer felt safe and made the decision to sell her house and move to Mansfield, where Billie lived. M.O. had been killed in a bank robbery and Billie lived alone with Nan and Georgia living nearby with their young families.

Big Mama had lived in the house on Confederate Avenue for over fifty years and we all thought that it was going to kill her to have to pack everything she owned and move at the age of 85!!! But we never took into consideration how strong and resilient this lady really was.

She bought a small cottage and Jack suggested some modifications while Billie helped with the painting and finding labor to accomplish the necessary repairs/renovations. Very soon that little cottage was a doll house. It had a screened porch on one side that she could sit and visit with mama, Mimi, family and visitors. The kitchen was perfect and she still had a back porch for her pantry. The front room spanned the width of the house and Big Mama placed her living room furniture – complete with the glass shelves in the windows – on one end of the room and her dining room furniture on the end next to the porch.

Every weekend she would entertain company. She was delighted that her little cottage was THE meeting place for the family. Jack and Gert would come down from Gainesville, Sue and Bud would come over from Decatur, Mary would come down from Snellville, and Billie would come over from right down the street. She was so very happy.

Big Mama knew every individual in her family and she knew their most favorite food – and would prepare that dish every time that person came to visit her. That was her way of showing you that you were that special to her.

But everyone know that there was one person that was a little bit more special than everyone else (after Big Daddy was gone) and that was Jack. Every time Jack called to tell her that he and Gert were coming, Big Mama would start cooking.

Now, Bruce and I had the hardware store in Mansfield and Bruce would get wind of some deal or discount and pass it on to his family. And there was this egg farm outside town that sold eggs by the flat for a lot less than the super market. At that time I was also baking and decorating cakes to supplement our income and eggs were one of the big expenses, so I would go pick up flats of eggs weekly.

I asked Big Mama if she could use a whole flat of eggs and she got very excited. We all knew that she had so little coming in and she had so much going out – especially in groceries for all of her visitors... and that included me – so I lied. Yes, I lied to my Big Mama. I told her that the eggs were only fifty cents a flat. So, for the next couple of months, every other week I would swing by on my way home and drop off one or two flats and try to get out, but oh no!!! Big Mama was going to pay you what she owed you if she had to count it out in pennies on the spot!!! Yeah, it was costing me a little, but she really did enjoy her eggs.

Then, in the spring, Big Mama would call me to see if I could take her to pick up some eggs as she was expecting company, or she would ask me to get her three or four flats the next time. She knew a bargain and she knew how to make provisions stretch, so eggs were her mainstay. What she didn't know was that the hatchery went up on the price of their eggs, or sometimes they just would not have enough "seconds" to make enough flats for Big Mama's order and what I needed for my cakes... but I just could NOT deny her this and not deliver those eggs!

The Good Lord finally showed mercy on my lying soul and the hatchery quit selling eggs out right to anyone. Breaking the news to Big Mama was less awful than I had anticipated. I honestly believe that she got sick of eggs too.

And lessons in honesty were constant when you were around this precious woman. I remember going over one morning and as I was leaving she asked me to take her mail to the post office for her. I told her no problem, but on my way out the door I noticed the addresses on the envelopes; Billy Graham, Charles Stanley, and, oh no! Jim Baker.

I whirled around and shook that envelope at Big Mama and spluttered out something about the poor widow's mite being sent to the stinking rotten crook (my diplomacy was equal to my maturity at that time in my life) and "placed" that particular envelope back on her dining room table.

Big Mama quietly walked over to the envelope, picked it up and handed it back to me. Then with a look in her eye that defied further conversation she said, "God has given every man a duty to fulfill. To me, my duty is to be faithful. To this preacher, his duty is to serve his Master. Now, I can't control what this preacher does with his duty. But I certainly can and will do my duty. I will be faithful. Now thank you for taking this to the post office for me and come see me when you can."

'Nuf said.

Except that I yearn to see Big Mama again. And I will.

"What a day of rejoicing that will be....".

Thank you for listening to my ramblings, Jack. And thank you for compiling this history. You will always be my hero.

Love
Nan

XIV. Letter from Jack Butterworth's double first cousin <u>John Evans Butterworth</u> b. 1909 to his Grandson Michael James Caton 3-12-79

Dear Michael, I'm very sorry that I have been unable to write you before now. It's always a pleasure to hear from you and to do what I can to help you with your projects. I surely do miss you and always want to see you.

Well, here goes.

Q – What was it like when you were little?

A – When I was your age we lived in the small country town of Canton, GA. My father died when I was one year old and my mother died when I was six. This made me real sad. My older brother and sister and I lived with my grandfather and my Aunt (Mother's sister). They were real good to us. My grandfather raised and sold horses and mules and buggies. He had a real big house which he had built. It was on a very large lot and he had a large barn which accommodated six or eight horses with a loft above for store feed. There was another small barn in which he kept a cow (Bess). It was my job to go to the pasture some 2-3 miles away and lead her to the barn and milk her every afternoon. Grandpa taught me how to ride a horse. He was a great rider. He used to tell me to place his hat on the ground and would ride Indian style at a real fast speed reaching down and picking up his hat and giving a loud rebel yell. He had a large farm in the country where his daddy had built a house and barn. His father moved in on the farm area about the time the Cherokee Indians were driven out by the Government. My grandfather's uncle won a large tract of land when the Government took over the Cherokee Indian territory. Granddad's folks like the Indians and were very sorry about the way they were treated. (An Indian named Cherokee was buried on his property.)

Q – What kind of house did you live in?

A - I mentioned the second house which was a two story house with porches on the front and back and also a porch upstairs in the back. Two families lived there...both were his daughter's family. The house that I was born in was a single story house which was next door to the oldest house in Canton, GA. The old home was a Colonial mansion. During the Civil War a Mr. Galt, the owner of the fine home lived there. When the half crazed Gen. Sherman burned his way towards the sea he used Mr. Galt's home while in that area as his headquarters. He burned all of the houses and barns in that area except the Galt house. He left it standing when he moved on. But took everything of value. His army ate, stole or destroyed all of the livestock population in the path. The Galt descendents still live in the old mansion. According to them Mr. Galt was a mason and since Gen. Sherman was a mason he left the Galt house unburned. Mr. Galt was a business man and was in the Canton area when the land was taken from the Cherokee Indians and was divided into several counties. Mr. Galt wanted to start a silk business so he went to Canton, China and brought back some silk worms and set up a silk business at the back of his mansion. The people there decided to name the place Canton, GA. The silk business failed but the town retained the name Canton. They say that the climate there is a little too cold for silk worms. The house I was born in has another story added to it since I lived there. (Will send you pictures later) I had a lot of playmates both around home and in school. We had plenty of places to play near creeks and a river in the barns and in the fields. It was colder there than it is in Atlanta. In the winter time we would ride a sled down the sidewalk on a long hill in front of the house. The snow was clean and we made snow cream out of it with milk, sugar and vanilla. We also fished a lot.

Q – What kind of car did you have?

A – My grandfather did not own a car. He always had a nice buggy and fine horses. We either traveled this way or walked, rode a train. When he rented a car, a driver would come with it. The horns on the cars would go Ah-Uga, Ah-Uga. This would usually scare the horses.

Q – What kind of telephone did you have?

A – It was called a magneto type telephone. It looked like this. It was located on the wall a little higher than my head (then). You didn't dial numbers like you do today. The operator would get your number for you. To reach the operator you would raise the receiver and turn the crank. When the operator answered you would tell her through the transmitter who you wanted to talk to or what number you wanted. (Will send you a picture of this also.)

Q – Did you have a sewing machine?

A – Yes, almost every woman owned one. It was like a small piece of furniture with legs and small wheels or casters so that it could be moved about the room. The machine was run by foot power with the use of a foot pedal not with an electric motor.

Q – Tell about food.

A – We had an ice box which looked a little like a refrigerator today and even though we had electrical current there were no electric refrigerators at that time. We used ice to keep the food cold. The ice man would come about three times a week and leave about 50 lbs. per ice box. We cooked on a wood stove. There were no gas or electric stoves available. Grandpa would buy groceries in real large quantities because it was cheaper that way. Flour would come in barrels, sugar 50-100 lbs., potatoes 100 lbs., corn meal in real large sacks, bacon in sides, syrup by the gallons and we had large sacks of dried beans and peas. And in the summertime we had plenty of fresh vegetables of the garden.

Q – *What kind of clothes did you wear?*

A – *I wore knee length trousers and long black stockings reaching from my feet to my knees. In the winter time I wore heavy underwear and slept in a feather bed and in the summertime I wore light underwear and went barefooted.*

Michael, I will send you some pictures. Am sorry but when I hid the key to my file cabinet I hid it too good and now I can't find it. I hope this gives you an idea about my young life.

Lots of love,
Granddad

P. S. Hug everyone for me.

Written by J. Evans Butterworth to his grandson, Michael.

XV. Letter to daughters from Buena Vista Wilberth Evans ca 1904

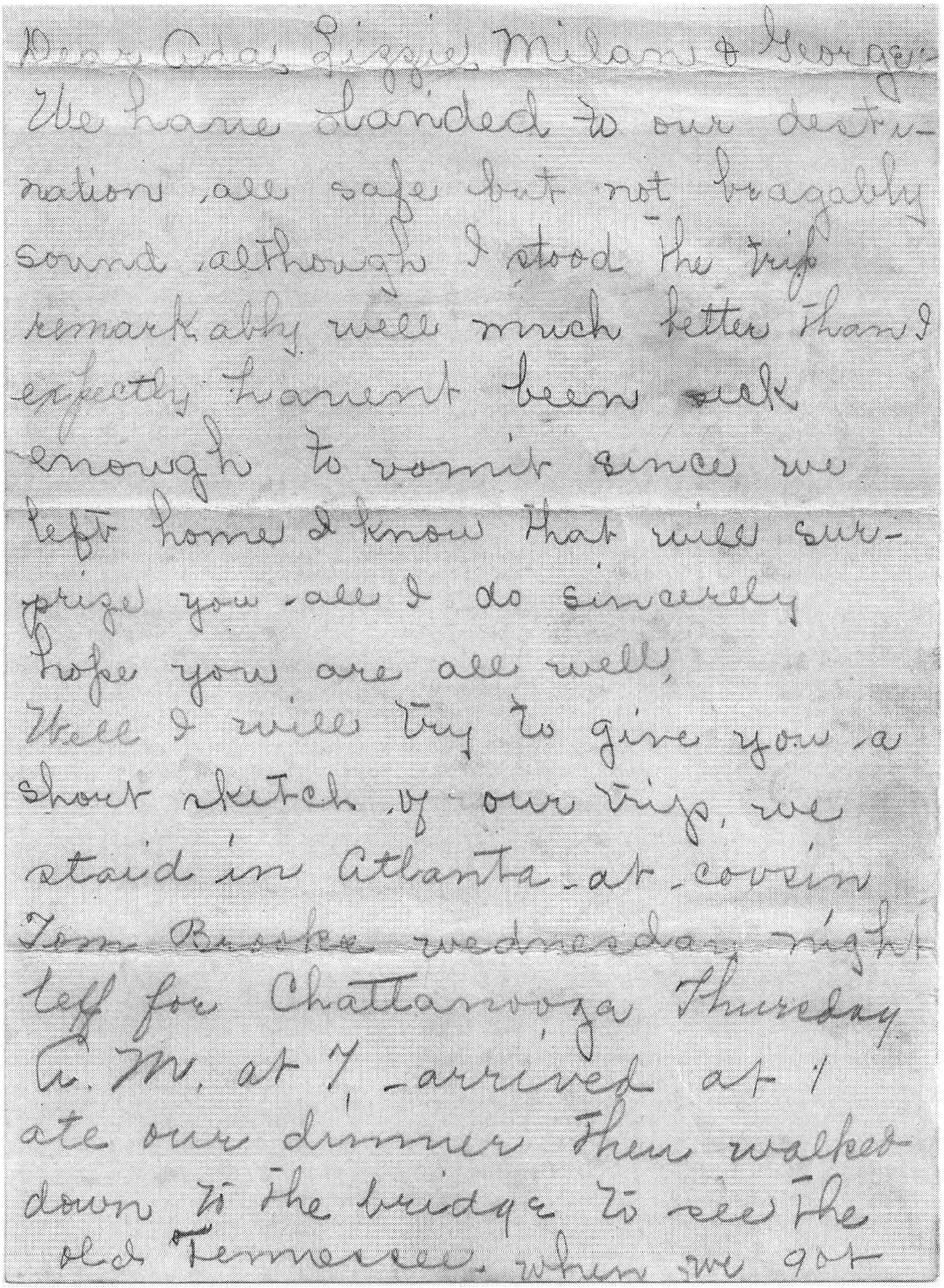

Dear Ada, Lizzie, Milam & George,
We have landed to our destination, all safe but not bragably sound although I stood the trip remarkably well much better than I expected, havent been sick enough to vomit since we left home I know that will surprize you all I do sincerely hope you are all well,
Well I will try to give you a short sketch of our trip, we staid in Atlanta at cousin Tom Brooks wednesday night left for Chattanooga Thursday A. M. at 7 arrived at 1 ate our dinner then walked down to the bridge to see the old Tennessee. when we got

Fig. 123   Letter of Trip to Arkansas by Buena Vista Wilberth Evans ca. 1904

back I felt like I would be as
easy pulled intoo about the middle
as a wasp then we took a car
and rode out to look-out moon
tain went to a little house
at the foot and got a very good
drink sit down & watched one car go
up & one go-down but the sight
caused my heart to fail me, in
venturing up, then we rode back
and left out for memphis
at 6 p. m. and traveled all
night only stopping a very few
moments at a time and arrived
at 6 a. m Friday started at half
past 7 to Little Rock crossed the
famous Mississippi and allow
me to call it I would say it was
a first cousin to the screw me

morning at half past seven
and started to Russelville and
landed at 10 Sat. morn. There
was a little car that run
down ½ miles to the Arkansas river then we got in a
Buss and rode across on
a Pontoon Bridge into
Dardenelle then hired a conveyen-
ce and drove out 4 miles in the
country to Mrs Marley who
married Emeline got out there
Sat evening about 2, Sunday
Morning we went out 3 miles
to New Hope church heard a man
by the name of Robinson preach
it was decoration day every
body brought there dinner

and his mother said they
never was so surprised
nor overjoyed in all their
lives tell Will I give him
credit for this trip and I
will never will stop praising
him untill the light has all
gone out in my eyes and
my tongue cease to speak
now I could write you all
day and not tell half but
they are hurrying me to
ride out several miles
in the country to the cemetary
your aunt Matilda
was burried to see if
we could find the grave
Trusting to God the kind

traveled for several miles down through water and over water seen any amount of houses with the water still all around them I tell you it was right trying on my Cowardize, after we got a little away from the water all we had to do was to look at fine farms The next river was St Francis, then Red then White, then to Fort Smith crossed the Arkansas river then we landed in Little Rock Friday about 2 oclock then got in car & rode all over business part of town, and stopped at Ozark house that night untill Saturday

and a lot of flowers and
decorated every graves in
the cemetary I expect there
was five hundred people there,
after dinner we drove about
5 miles in the Arkansas bottoms
your Cousin John said there
was ten thousand acres
then we went back to Emeline
and staid untill Monday
morning then started through
the country again about 20
miles W John Evans went
through Centerville crossed
the Petrejean river then to
Ola then to Fort Valley to
John's home he is certainly
well fixed up and him

father that you are all well I will close direct your letters to Gilkey Yell Co. Ark, and if any thing should happen bad let me know at once love to every one kiss the babys for me and write soon

Your Mother.

XVI. Memories written by Jim Newby Butterworth about his childhood days.

June 23, 2011

I have heard it said that the sense of smell is the primary sense that gives us memories of our life experiences. This has, certainly, been true for me. I am convinced that my first memory in life took place in the springtime in Marietta, Georgia, when I was not much more than an infant. Family history tells me that my father, Jackson Evans Butterworth, Sr., my mother, Gertrude Newby Butterworth, and my brother, Jackson Evans Butterworth, Jr., lived on Vance Circle. My first memory took place, probably, in the front or back yard of that residence on a warm, sunny spring morning. I can feel still the warmth of the morning sun, but the smell that I remember is overpowering. It is unmistakable, and I seek it out and relish it every spring to this date. The smell is best described as a sweet but musky smell. The plant is an evergreen that has profuse white blossoms about April or May. Nurseries today have a new name for the plant, and it has been modified and cross bred to some degree, but still the same flowers and same aroma occur each spring. Regardless of the changes in names and slight change in leaves, I still refer to the plant as privet hedge.

From Marietta, my family moved to Hodgson Drive in Athens, Georgia, probably in about 1946. The street address was 305. In his later years, my Dad told me that when the family was moving from Marietta to Athens, it was necessary for him to travel by himself to Athens to get established for a couple of weeks. He told me that he resided in the old Georgian Hotel for those days. Dad moved to Athens to work for a Marble and Granite company where he designed monuments and tombstones, just as he had in Marietta, Atlanta, and Winnsboro, South Carolina prior to my birth.

My memories in Athens are wonderful. My brother Jackie and I shared a bedroom on the back side of the house, and only a few steps from the kitchen area where I learned to enjoy scrambled eggs with syrup on top and toast with lots of butter and only slightly toasted. Our dear black maid and I referred to the toast as "easy toast". Annie was a part of our family. Looking back at our times in Athens, it is clear that we loved and respected Annie, and she loved us.

Childhood memories abound during the Athens time. I recall: Going to the YMCA with my brother, going to the movie with my brother, playing with my friend Freddie Bell in the backyard and in a vacant lot next door, where there was large boulders, meeting my Dad at the end of the driveway when he came home from work so that I could ride to the top of the driveway with him, playing with toy cars in the front yard and meeting (perhaps for the first time) my cousin Newby, who came to Athens to go to the University of Georgia.

Beyond the memories I have mentioned, another stands out, and it involves again the sense of smell. It became a practice for a time for my mother to prepare herself to go downtown Athens and go shopping. Of necessity, I would be taken with her. She and I would walk a half a block or so and catch a bus to downtown Athens. Unlike today, ladies would dress to go shopping. Mom would wear a dress, a hat, and gloves. On the particular day that I recall, I was busying myself looking through the perfume bottles in Mom's room. I could hold the bottle to my eye and see a magnificent red color. While seeking this color, I would smell the perfume that was so familiar. I don't know the name of the perfume, but feel rather sure that if I could find it, I would again recognize the smell.

We moved to 301 North Bradford Street, Gainesville, Georgia, when I was about five years old. The house was an absolute joy for any child. It had a cellar with windows on one side that allowed some sun into that area. A great place to play. The back stairs rose and turned a time or two to a lattice back area that went into the kitchen. The kitchen joined a large room, which probably had been a dining room, but which we used for virtually everything including our first television set. In that room there was also a heater that might have been a wood heater, perhaps a coal heater. Regardless, Mom stoked the heater primarily with rolled up newspaper which, in a few minutes, could turn the thin metal of the heater to a rosy red. In the winter, most areas outside this room were quite frosty, but I don't think any of us really gave much thought to that.

The entrance to the front of the house at 301 North Bradford was up several wooden steps to a porch that fronted most the house. Upon coming in the front door, there was a large area with a staircase going to the next level of the house. To the right was a room that probably was a parlor, and to the left were sliding "pocket" doors that were secured to cordon off the other side of the house where the Gibbons family lived.

In those early years in Gainesville, my Dad worked for Gainesville Marble Company. Mom continued her teaching career, which eventually spanned at least four decades in Gainesville. I think Jack was in the 5th grade when we moved to Gainesville, and he continued his adventures through Candler Street Elementary School, Gainesville High School and then on to Emory University and Medical College of Georgia. My brother has always been a hard act to follow. Not that we were competitive. Jack excelled in all areas: Honor student, Beta Club, Key Club, Eagle Scout, musician, athlete, soldier and physician. The best brother anyone could ever have.

The smells that I recall during this Gainesville period don't come from Gainesville. During this Gainesville time, the family took regular trips to Atlanta and Vienna. It was not unusual for us all to climb into our 1941 black four door Plymouth and travel to Atlanta on any given Sunday. We would make a couple of stops, going to Confederate Avenue to see my Dad's parents (my grandparents Virgil and George Butterworth) and then to "Bit and Kelly's" house. My Grandmother was given her father's name - George, but was known to all of us as "Big Mama". The name "Big Mama" was fitting, and I will say no more about that. On the other hand, my Grandfather was known as "Big Daddy", which really was not the case. He was a slim fellow, maybe six feet tall, with a shiny bald crown and those old-fashioned round spectacles. He would read us the funny papers while we sat on a sofa in their parlor, the sofa being the same that later inhabited my parents' living room.

Big Mama would prepare an elaborate noon meal. Often times, a roast, potatoes, gravy, beans and what I now know to be a great Sunday dinner. As a child, the meal did not appeal very much. After the Sunday meal, the children would play some games such as Chinese checkers or Mr. Potato Head. We would conclude our visit with everyone sitting on the back screened porch, where aunts and uncles and cousins from the neighborhood would have gathered for their Sunday time.

On leaving Confederate Avenue, we would travel to 631 Claremont Avenue in Decatur to visit with Bit and Kelly Pharr, Mom's sister and brother-in-law. The Pharrs had four children. The oldest child being Johnny my childhood buddy. There was then Will, Phil and Royce.

The smell that I remember from these Atlanta trips comes from Big Mama's kitchen. I did not see it as a pleasant smell at the time. It was a heavy, greasy, steamy smell of a lot of food being prepared. Regardless, it is a smell of memory and one that I now recognize as a good southern Sunday dinner.

Trips to Vienna were high points in my childhood. Memories of aromas are almost too numerous to recall. The aromas are so intense that I can, with concentration, close my eyes and transport myself to those earlier days. Here is a list of just some of the smells: Jonquils and narcissus in the hallway leading into my Grandmother's house; a certain soap that was mixed by Charity in a bucket to mop the wooden floors of the house; the salt cured ham hanging in a small room adjacent to the kitchen; Juicy Fruit chewing gum hidden in the dresser drawer of my Aunt Minnie and sparingly shared with my cousin Johnny; a smell at the soda fountain of my Uncle Joe's drug store, one that I cannot describe, but which was pleasant and I would easily recognize again; the smell of snuff, I believe "Dental Sweet Snuff", in my Grandmother's bedroom. (I will not divulge the user of this snuff); smells at Christmas that were a collection of candy smells, new leather billfolds or cowboy boot smells, Christmas tree smells and an aroma from a newly opened Lifesaver candy book, with Lifesavers of each flavor displayed under cellophane. To conclude this trip down memory lane, I will describe a typical Christmas trip to Vienna, at least as I recall it. About two weeks before Christmas, while we were still in Gainesville, I would begin to count down the days. I would listen to WGGA, where Santa Claus would read letters each afternoon. I also spent considerable time going through the Sears Roebuck catalog analyzing the various toys available. As the days counted down, the excitement increased. Two weeks turned to one week, and then only a few days before Santa would come. We would leave Gainesville to travel to Vienna for Christmas as soon as my Dad could get away from his work. This might be a day or so before Christmas Eve. It was more common than not that we would leave in the dark of the night, having packed our four-door Plymouth with suitcases, presents, toys, our pet Chihuahua, food, blankets, and the list goes on. Dad would drive, Mom would sit in the right front seat with something under her feet, and Jack and I would tussle in the back seat. Early on, I was small enough to fit on the shelf under the back window. We would usually carry our food for the trip, as restaurants were few and far between, and I expect we did not need the expense of stopping.

On arriving in Vienna, we were greeted as celebrities. Aunt Minnie, Aunt Alice, Uncle Joe, my Grandmother Burr, Robert, Jr., Melissa, perhaps Aunt Sity and Uncle Jack, Bit and Kelly and their children, and the list goes on. Everyone was overjoyed to see their "folks".

Christmas Eve day lasted forever. We had a big breakfast of biscuits and gravy, country ham, scrambled eggs, grits, sausage and, perhaps, some brains and eggs (but not for me). Burr would drink her coffee after pouring it into her saucer, and she would eat streak-o-lean while being chided by her daughters that such was unhealthy. Firecrackers were always a must around Christmas. My cousin Johnny and I tried to explode as many as possible in the front yard of Burr's house. On one occasion, we managed to drop a cherry bomb onto the windshield of Robert, Jr.'s new (I think 1957) Chrysler automobile. Robert, Jr., was an observer; and when he saw the windshield break, his only response was, "damn", and with that he went into the house.

Johnny and I would wake up on our pallet under the dining room table. We started our Christmas day as early as possible. Santa Claus came to the children in the front hallway of Burr's house. Our stockings were filled with walnuts, pecans and other nuts, the names of which are no longer in vogue. We also got caps for our cap pistols, tangerines, firecrackers, and chewing gum. Each item and morsel was treasured.

Later in the day, we opened presents in the front room known as the parlor. The only access to this room was from a door on the front porch, and this always seemed odd to me. The room would be packed with every relative known, and the excitement, joy, joking and confusion was at an all time fever pitch. To bring these notes to a conclusion, let me talk about my Grandmother, Viola Newby. She was the center of all the cooking, flowers and Christmas activities. Far beyond that, she was the magnet that made Vienna so important to me. She always seemed a frail lady, and I don't really know how old she was as I was a child and growing up. She wore simple clothes, always dresses. On those few occasions when I saw her "dressed up", she would wear hats, sometimes with a net veil. I believe that she probably made most of her clothes. Most of her "dress clothes" were purple. She spent much time sitting at her sewing machine, one with a foot treadle. There would often times be tissue paper dress patterns around her room. She was always gracious, loving and warm to all the children. She engaged us in talk and activities. She kept us busy. She would entice us to turn the crank on the ice cream machine on the back porch or go down along the train track to pick blackberries so she could make blackberry jelly. In the summer, she always had a can of paint and some brushes available so that we could be "permitted" to paint outside furniture. The only discipline that she rendered as I recall was on those occasions when Johnny and I would run through her bedroom area. On about the third or fourth occasion, after having been told to stop running, Burr would take one of her needles, hold it so that only about an eighth of the needle protruded past her fingers and stick us in the butt as we ran by. If this was, in fact, discipline, it was met by all of us with a laugh and an ouch. We loved Burr very much.

I could go on and on with chapters on my adolescent days in Gainesville, my teenage meanderings, my North Georgia College adventures, and life thereafter. Maybe all of that for another time.

James Newby Butterworth 4/16/2011

June 23, 2011

Our family had been living at 301 North Bradford for a year or two. I was only six or seven years old, but I had freedom to explore anywhere within several blocks. A bicycle was my means of transportation, and I roamed from the Western Auto Store on the south side of the square to the Imperial Drug Store on the square and onto the old Coca Cola Building next to Hermie Johnson's house.

In the course of my travels, I often passed on the sidewalk of Bradford across from the side of the Big Star Grocery. There I passed Toy Minor's Meat Market and then Parks' Feed Store. Mrs. Parks had a beauty shop in the back of the feed store. The store was a good place to buy a couple of pieces of one cent Bazooka bubble gum.

Between Toy Minor's and Parks' was a stairway that lead to the second floor room above Toy Minor's. One afternoon as I passed the stairway, I heard piano music - floating literally from above. I was entranced. I snuck up the stairway listening for more music when I saw the sign "piano lessons". Our family had inherited a piano when we moved to 301. Clearly, the previous occupant of 301 had decided to abandon the piano. It was a large rectangular rosewood piano that set in the front room of the house. The piano worked, and I had become ready to learn. When I got home from my adventure up the stairway, I broke the news to my mother: I wanted to take music lessons. Mom was happy; and within a few days, I was climbing the stairs to take my first lesson. I was shown Middle C and how to hold my fingers on the keys. Up and down the scale, time and time again, I really got the hang of it. I learned F A C E and "Every Good Boy Does Fine". I practiced at home and learned "The Volga Boat Man". But my interest waned, and I practiced less and less. I concentrated less on the music before me and began to improvise, thinking perhaps it was meant for me to be a composer rather than just reading someone else's music. On these occasions and on hearing my renditions, Mom would appear in the room and ask, "what are you playing?" She did not seem to really like "my" music. As afternoons of practice and lessons passed, my teacher advised me that my first recital was scheduled. Electricity in the form of fear went through my entire body. What was a recital? Who would be there? What would I play? My teacher gave me the date of the recital and a sheet of music that I was to learn. I was directed to sit next to the window in her music studio and copy the sheet music. As I sat next to the window with afternoon yellow lights streaming onto the sheet music, I did my best to copy the music. I struggled to follow the lines and the squiggly notes and signs. After what seemed like hours, my teacher looked at my work - and laughed heartily. I had copied the same line of the music over and over. Embarrassed and crying, I left the teacher's studio, never to return and never to attend a recital.

But, days were good and back to my bicycle and back to my tours around town. Back to riding a circuit around the parking lot at Big Star and, oh happy day, to riding in a parade around the square. My bike decorated with colorful crepe paper ribbons and with playing cards clicking out a motor sound from my spokes.

Fig. 124   James Newby Butterworth ca. 1961

References

- The Butterworth Family of Maryland and Virginia- Walter V. Ball December 1960
- The History of Cherokee County (Georgia) –Rev. Lloyd G. Marlin 1932
- Remberts *By Way of* South Carolina- Sallie Henrietta Rembert, L.A. "Brooks" McCall 1979
- Key and Related Families- Mrs. Julian C. Lane 1931
- The History of Pittsylvania County Virginia- Maude Carter Clement 1981
- Carolina Cradle-Robert W. Ramsey 1964
- Notes on Some Families of Butterworth- David Butterworth 1995
- "Benjamin Franklin McCollum and the Home Guard"- Mashburn Collection Website
- *History of Gwinnett County, 1818-1960, Volume II,* by James C. Flanigan, copyright 1959
- The 31st Alabama Infantry Regiment-http://www.archives.alabama.gov/referenc/alamilor/31stinf.html
- Origin of the Name Butterworth-http://www.butterworths-int.co.uk/Anthology/Name%20Origin.htm
- The Scots-Irish A Social History. James Leyburn 1962

Made in the USA
Lexington, KY
03 August 2018